KEY TO MAP SYMBOLS

- ○ Cities with fewer than 100,000 people
- • Cities with 100,00 to 1,000,000 people
- ⊙ Cities with 1,000,000 people or more
- □ Capitals with fewer than 100,000 people
- ■ Capitals with 100,000 to 1,000,000 people
- ▣ Capitals with 1,000,000 or more people
- ★ State or provincial capitals
- ▲ Mountains or high points

All capitals of countries are in bold type.

Editor: Jennifer Justice
Editorial assistant: Claire Berridge
Designer: Heather Gough
Cover design: Smiljka Surla
Illustrations: Stephen Conlin, Jonathan Adams, Deborah Kindred, Swanston Graphics, Kevin Maddison, Claire Littlejohn, Hardlines, Tracy Wayte

Flags supplied by Lovell Johns, Oxford. Authenticated by the Flag Research Center, Winchester, Mass. 01890, USA

Note: At the time of going to press, the borders of Yugoslavia are uncertain. Bosnia Herzegovina and Macedonia had recently declared independence. Montenegro had voted to remain with Serbia, as part of the new Yugoslavia.

First published in 1992 by Grisewood & Dempsey Ltd,
Elsley House, 24-30 Great Titchfield Street, London W1P 7AD
Some of the maps in this edition were previously published by Kingfisher Books in the *Children's World Atlas* in 1987.

© Grisewood & Dempsey Ltd 1987, 1992

All rights reserved. No part of this publication may be reproduced, stored in a retrieval system or transmitted by any means, electronic, mechanical, photocopying or otherwise, without the prior permission of the publisher.

ISBN 0 906 279 98 4

Printed and bound in Italy

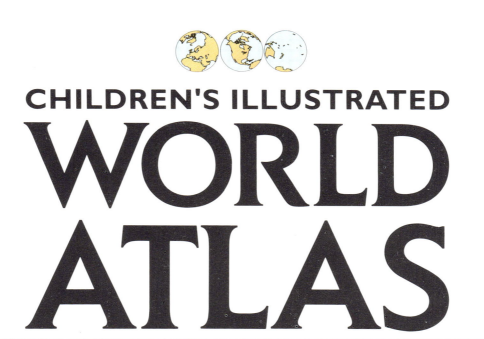

CHILDREN'S ILLUSTRATED
WORLD ATLAS

Philip Boys

Contents

Countries of the World	8
The Continents	10

EUROPE

The British Isles	12
France and Monaco	14
The Iberian Peninsula	16
Italy and its Neighbours	18
The Balkans and Romania	20
The Low Countries	22
Scandinavia and Finland	24
Germany, Switzerland and Austria	26
Poland, Czechoslovakia and Hungary	28
Russia and its Neighbours	30

ASIA

The Middle East	32
India and its Neighbours	34
China and its Neighbours	36
Japan	38
Southeast Asia	40

NORTH AMERICA

Canada	42
The United States	44
Mexico, Central America and the Caribbean	48

SOUTH AMERICA

The Andean Countries	50
Brazil and its Neighbours	52
Argentina and its Neighbours	54

AFRICA

North Africa	56
West Africa	58
Central and East Africa	60
Southern Africa	62

OCEANIA

Australia	64
New Zealand and the Pacific	66
The Polar Lands	68

FACTS AND FIGURES

The Earth: Facts and Figures	70
Index	71

Countries of the World

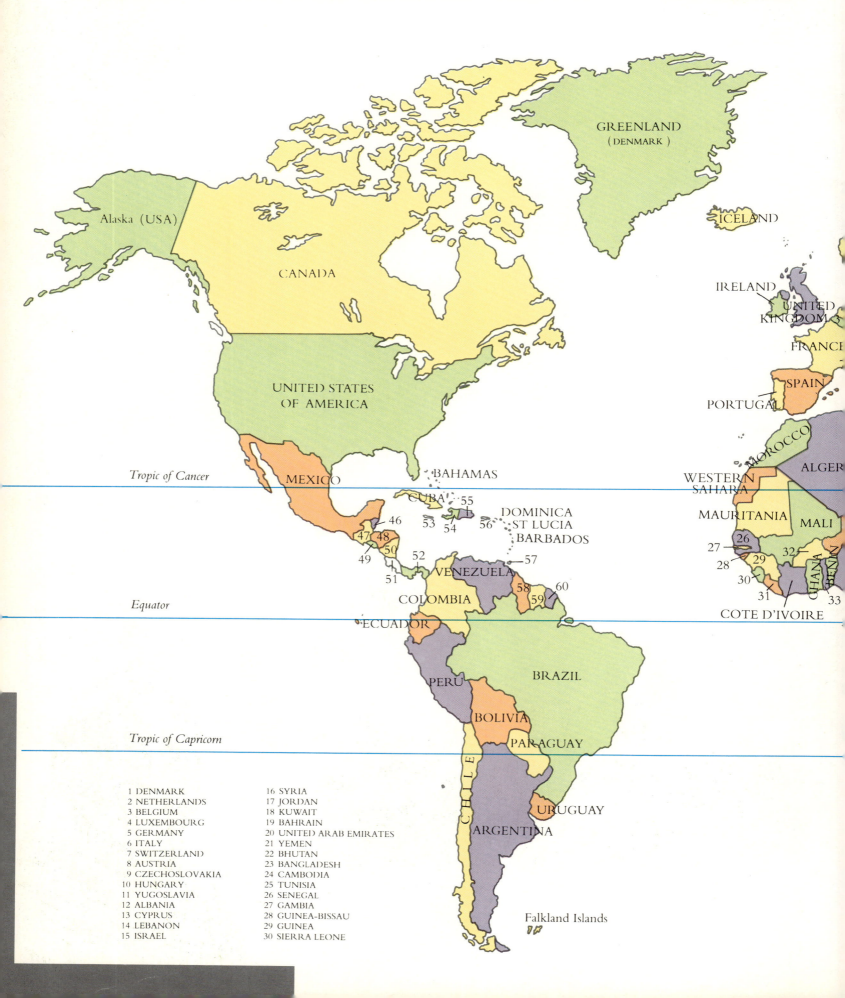

1 DENMARK
2 NETHERLANDS
3 BELGIUM
4 LUXEMBOURG
5 GERMANY
6 ITALY
7 SWITZERLAND
8 AUSTRIA
9 CZECHOSLOVAKIA
10 HUNGARY
11 YUGOSLAVIA
12 ALBANIA
13 CYPRUS
14 LEBANON
15 ISRAEL
16 SYRIA
17 JORDAN
18 KUWAIT
19 BAHRAIN
20 UNITED ARAB EMIRATES
21 YEMEN
22 BHUTAN
23 BANGLADESH
24 CAMBODIA
25 TUNISIA
26 SENEGAL
27 GAMBIA
28 GUINEA-BISSAU
29 GUINEA
30 SIERRA LEONE

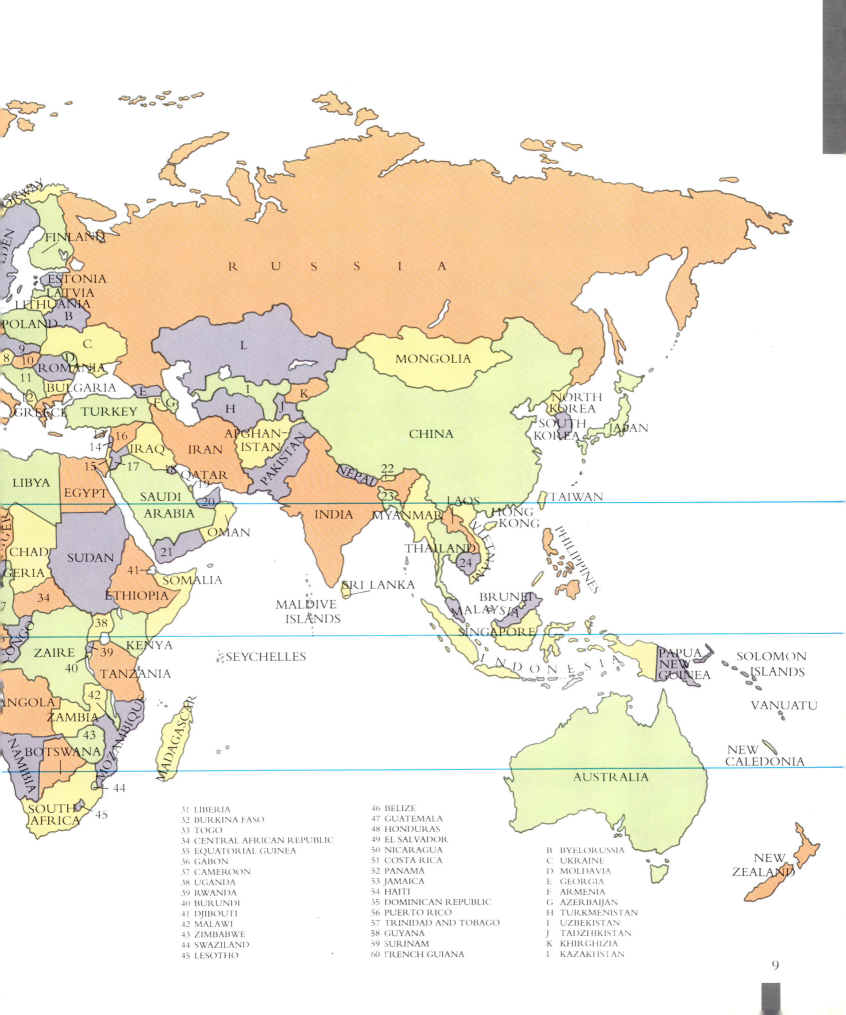

The Continents

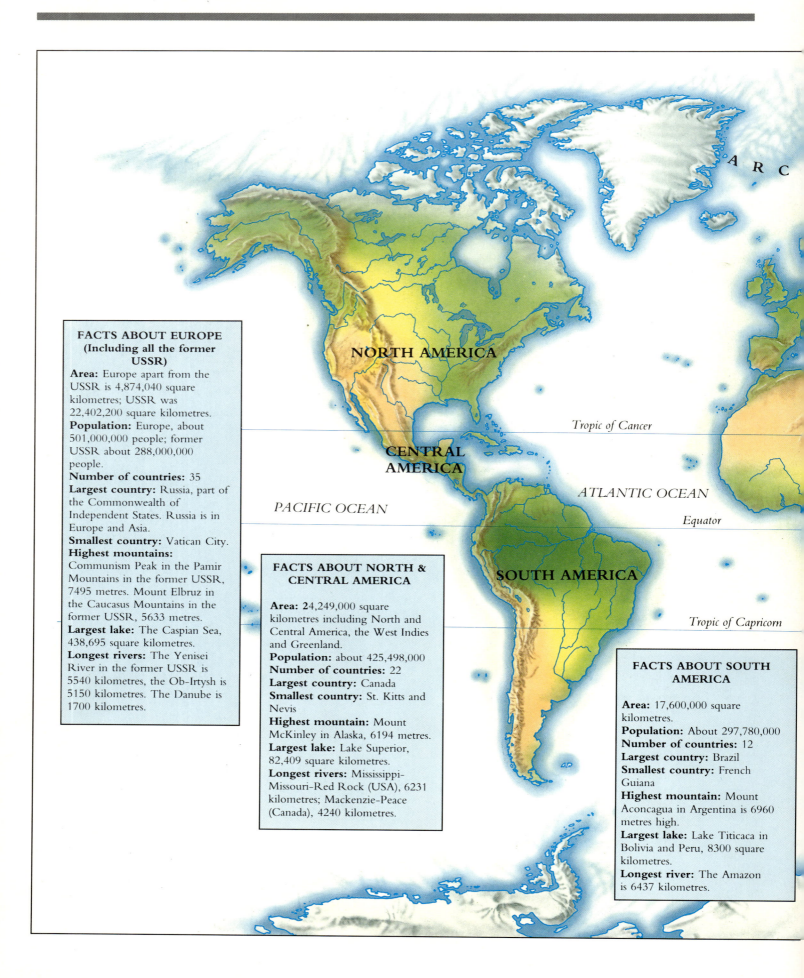

FACTS ABOUT EUROPE (Including all the former USSR)
Area: Europe apart from the USSR is 4,874,040 square kilometres; USSR was 22,402,200 square kilometres.
Population: Europe, about 501,000,000 people; former USSR about 288,000,000 people.
Number of countries: 35
Largest country: Russia, part of the Commonwealth of Independent States. Russia is in Europe and Asia.
Smallest country: Vatican City.
Highest mountains: Communism Peak in the Pamir Mountains in the former USSR, 7495 metres. Mount Elbruz in the Caucasus Mountains in the former USSR, 5633 metres.
Largest lake: The Caspian Sea, 438,695 square kilometres.
Longest rivers: The Yenisei River in the former USSR is 5540 kilometres, the Ob-Irtysh is 5150 kilometres. The Danube is 1700 kilometres.

FACTS ABOUT NORTH & CENTRAL AMERICA
Area: 24,249,000 square kilometres including North and Central America, the West Indies and Greenland.
Population: about 425,498,000
Number of countries: 22
Largest country: Canada
Smallest country: St. Kitts and Nevis
Highest mountain: Mount McKinley in Alaska, 6194 metres.
Largest lake: Lake Superior, 82,409 square kilometres.
Longest rivers: Mississippi-Missouri-Red Rock (USA), 6231 kilometres; Mackenzie-Peace (Canada), 4240 kilometres.

FACTS ABOUT SOUTH AMERICA
Area: 17,600,000 square kilometres.
Population: About 297,780,000
Number of countries: 12
Largest country: Brazil
Smallest country: French Guiana
Highest mountain: Mount Aconcagua in Argentina is 6960 metres high.
Largest lake: Lake Titicaca in Bolivia and Peru, 8300 square kilometres.
Longest river: The Amazon is 6437 kilometres.

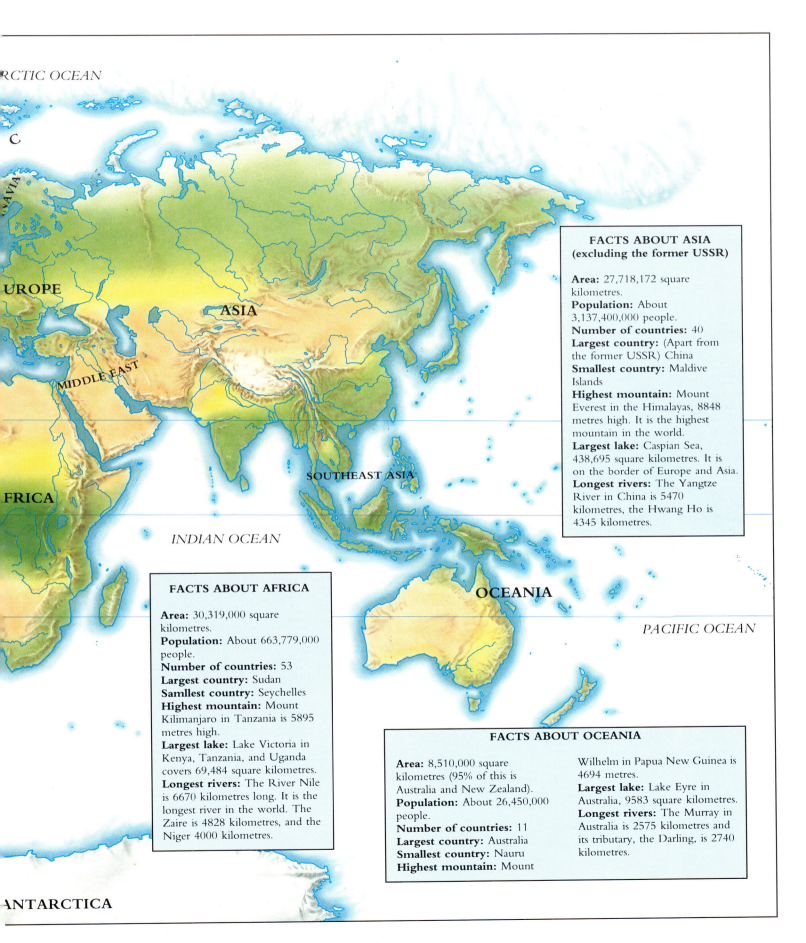

ARCTIC OCEAN

EUROPE

ASIA

MIDDLE EAST

AFRICA

SOUTHEAST ASIA

INDIAN OCEAN

OCEANIA

PACIFIC OCEAN

ANTARCTICA

FACTS ABOUT ASIA
(excluding the former USSR)

Area: 27,718,172 square kilometres.
Population: About 3,137,400,000 people.
Number of countries: 40
Largest country: (Apart from the former USSR) China
Smallest country: Maldive Islands
Highest mountain: Mount Everest in the Himalayas, 8848 metres high. It is the highest mountain in the world.
Largest lake: Caspian Sea, 438,695 square kilometres. It is on the border of Europe and Asia.
Longest rivers: The Yangtze River in China is 5470 kilometres, the Hwang Ho is 4345 kilometres.

FACTS ABOUT AFRICA

Area: 30,319,000 square kilometres.
Population: About 663,779,000 people.
Number of countries: 53
Largest country: Sudan
Samllest country: Seychelles
Highest mountain: Mount Kilimanjaro in Tanzania is 5895 metres high.
Largest lake: Lake Victoria in Kenya, Tanzania, and Uganda covers 69,484 square kilometres.
Longest rivers: The River Nile is 6670 kilometres long. It is the longest river in the world. The Zaire is 4828 kilometres, and the Niger 4000 kilometres.

FACTS ABOUT OCEANIA

Area: 8,510,000 square kilometres (95% of this is Australia and New Zealand).
Population: About 26,450,000 people.
Number of countries: 11
Largest country: Australia
Smallest country: Nauru
Highest mountain: Mount Wilhelm in Papua New Guinea is 4694 metres.
Largest lake: Lake Eyre in Australia, 9583 square kilometres.
Longest rivers: The Murray in Australia is 2575 kilometres and its tributary, the Darling, is 2740 kilometres.

The British Isles

The British Isles lie just off the coast of mainland Europe. They consist of the United Kingdom (England, Wales, Scotland and Northern Ireland) and the Republic of Ireland. Ireland was once part of the UK but it became independent in 1921.

Because there are warm ocean currents, the surrounding seas never ice over. The climate is generally mild and moist, but there are regional variations. The islands and highlands of the north and west are mostly mountainous, damp and cool. Forestry and of sheep and cattle farming are the main agricultural activities. The south and east are warmer and drier, and the land flatter and more fertile. Here wheat, vegetables, fruit and dairy produce are farmed, though a lot of food is also imported from abroad. Today, not many people live and work on the farms.

About 200 years ago, Britain was known as the "Workshop of the World", because its factory-made goods were sold in many parts of the world. New industrial cities grew up, particularly where there were coalfields to supply fuel or good harbours.

Many of the older and more traditional industries, such as shipbuilding and coal mining, have now declined. Today, new high technology industries and financial services (especially banking and insurance), are more important.

▲ *Far off the east coast of Scotland, immense rigs extract oil from deep below the North Sea. Conditions are dangerous, but oil is precious.*

◄ *Scotland's beautiful Grampian mountains include Ben Nevis, the UK's highest peak (1347 m). Rain is frequent and heavy here.*

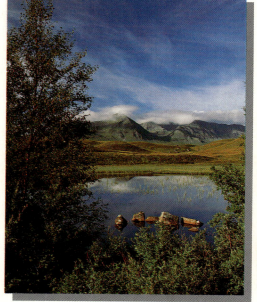

▲ *Two thousand years ago, the Romans built a walled town on the north bank of the River Thames and a narrow wooden bridge. The site they chose was the small hill on which St Paul's Cathedral now stands. Eventually, London grew to be a major world city.*

Country	Republic of Ireland (Eire)	United Kingdom
Capital	Dublin	London
Area (sq km)	70,285	244,100
Population	3,503,000	57,335,000
Official language	English, Irish	English

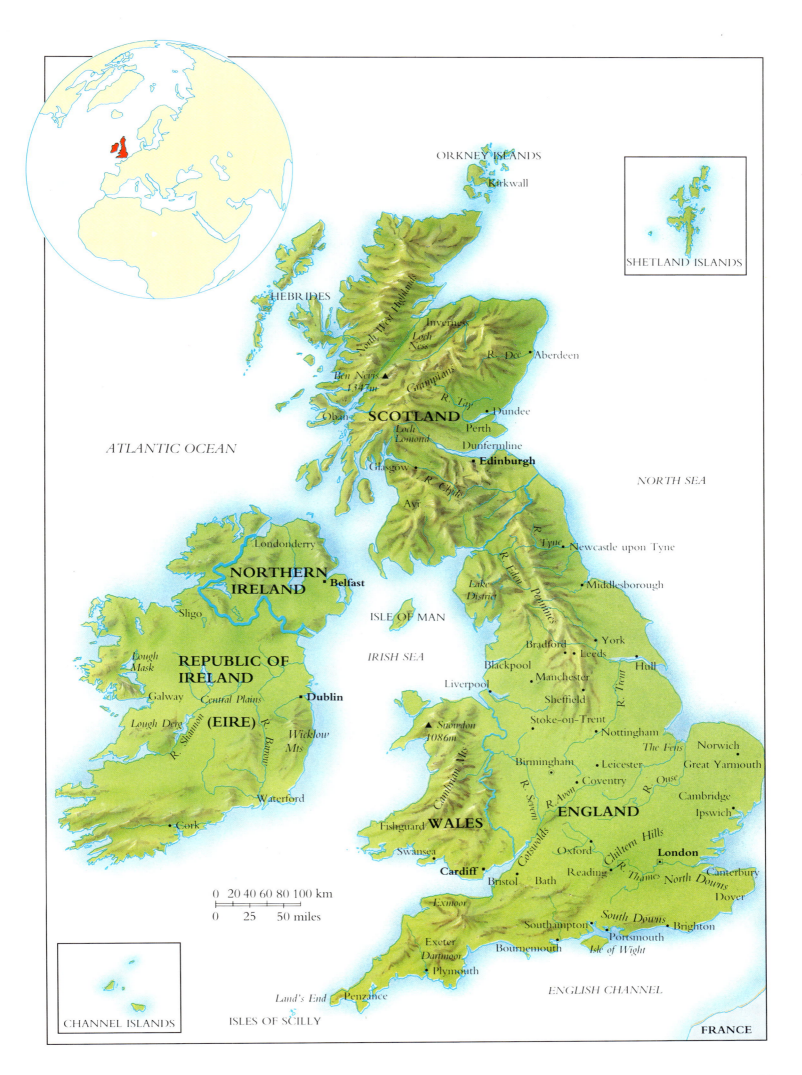

France and Monaco

France is larger than any other European country except Russia. It also has the most varied landscape and climates. The south is hot and dry but the north is often cool and wet. France also has some spectacular mountain ranges, such as the Pyrenees along its borders with Spain and the Alps and Juras in the southeast.

Rivers have always been important for the transport of people and goods. Great cities have grown up along their banks. These include Lyon on the River Rhône and Strasbourg on the River Rhine! France's capital, Paris, is on the River Seine.

France produces a great range of food and drink. For example, there are over 300 different cheeses, including such well-known varieties as Camembert, Roquefort and Brie. Every also produces its own special wine. The famous red wine known as claret originates from grapes grown in the area around Bordeaux. Its "bubbly" white wine, champagne, comes from the region to the east of Paris.

France is also a great industrial nation, producing cars and many other manufactured goods. But there is little coal or oil, so most of its electricity now comes from nuclear power. There are more than 40 nuclear power stations, chiefly sited on coastlines away from the cities or along France's borders with Germany and Luxembourg.

▲ *Tiny Monaco's world-famous casino. Other attractions include a marina and Grand Prix racing.*

▲ *Chateau Meursault, near Dijon. Many French wines are named after the chateau or great house in whose vineyards they are grown.*

Country	France	Monaco
Capital	Paris	Monte Carlo
Area (sq km)	547,026	1.9
Population	56,440,000	29,000
Official language	French	French

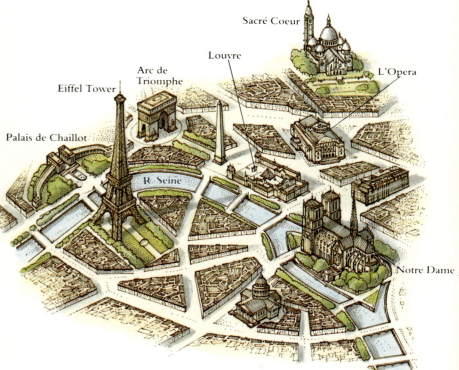

▲ *France's great city, Paris, started life 2500 years ago as a village on a tiny island in the River Seine. The great cathedral of Notre Dame was built there in 1163. Paris has grown in every direction, but the island and cathedral remain at its heart.*

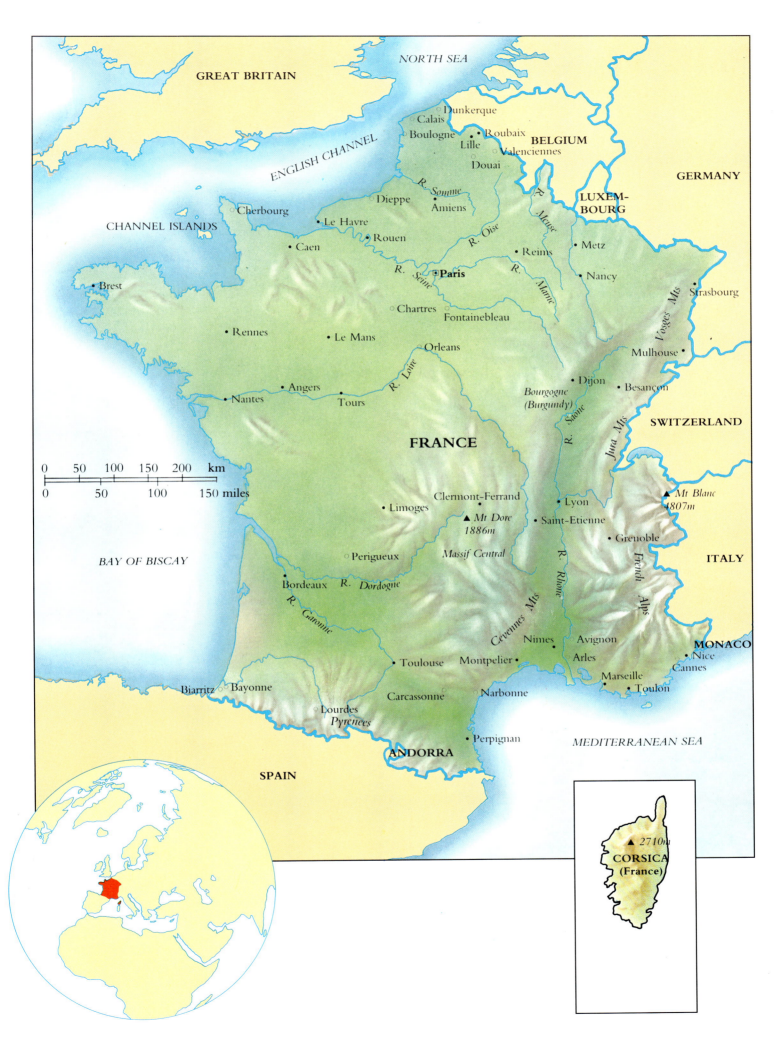

The Iberian Peninsula

Spain and Portugal are located on a square-shaped peninsula in the extreme southwest of Europe. They are very hot and dry in the summer, but can be bitterly cold in the winter. Much of the region is mountainous. Olives and grapes are grown almost everywhere. The region is famous for its full-bodied red wines and for fortified (extra strong) wines such as port, which comes from the area around Oporto, and sherry, named after Jerez, an area near Cadiz.

Throughout history, most of Portugal's population has lived close to the sea. The land is often more fertile here. It was also possible to earn a living by fishing or trading goods. Sardines are the most important catch. Spain has a long tradition of iron- and steel-making. In earlier times, guns and swords were the main products. Today it is automobiles.

In the last 30 years, tourism has boomed, especially along the sunny south-facing coastlines. The most popular areas are the Algarve in Portugal, and the various costas ("coasts") along Spain's Mediterranean shores. These include the Costa del Sol ("Sunny Coast") and Costa Blanca ("White Coast").

In the south, Gibraltar is only 14 km from Africa. The British set up a fortress here in 1704. It is still a British colony, though Spain wants to make Gibraltar part of its territory.

▲ *With its excellent road, rail, air and sea links with France and the rest of Europe, Barcelona is thriving as an industrial and cultural centre.*

▲ *The ancient hilltop castle at Sintra, close to Portugal's capital Lisbon, was built more than 1000 years ago by Muslims or "Moors" from North Africa.*

Country	Andorra	Gibraltar (UK)	Portugal	Spain
Capital	Andorra la Vella	Gibraltar	Lisbon	Madrid
Area (sq km)	453	6.0	91,985	504,750
Population	52,000	31,000	10,525,000	38,959,000
Official language	Catalan	English	Portuguese	Spanish

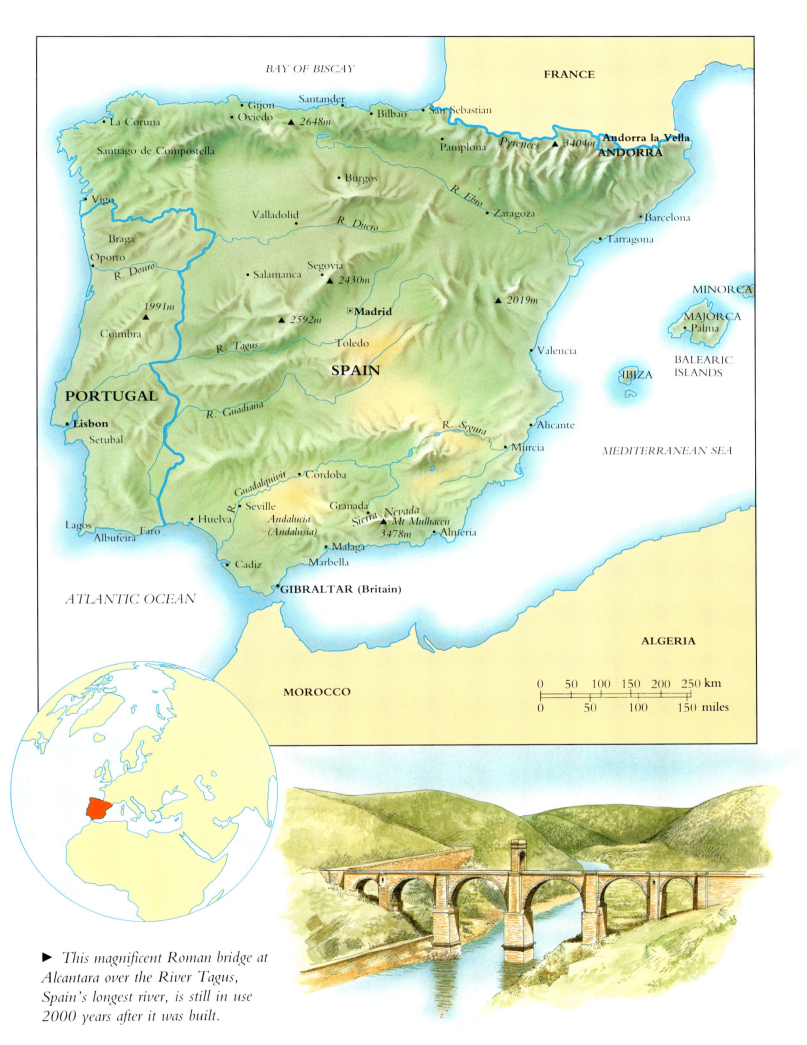

▶ This magnificent Roman bridge at Alcantara over the River Tagus, Spain's longest river, is still in use 2000 years after it was built.

Italy and its Neighbours

The shape of Italy is very easy to identify. From space, it looks like a boot kicking a ball (the island of Sicily). Italy is a mountainous country. The Alps separate Italy from northern Europe, and a chain of mountains, the Apennines, forms a "backbone" down its length.

Earthquakes are quite common in the south, and there are several active volcanoes. The most infamous of these is Mt Vesuvius. In AD 79 it erupted and buried the towns of Pompeii and Herculaneum beneath many metres of ash and boiling mud.

The largest area of flat land is the wide fertile valley of the River Po in the north. Most of Italy's people, industry and agriculture are located here. Cars and fashionable clothes are important products. Thanks to the many fast-flowing rivers that drain into the Po valley from the Alps, much of northern Italy's electricity can be generated by hydro-power. Vatican City, the centre of the Roman Catholic Church, is a tiny independent state in the middle of Rome, Italy's capital.

The hot, dry south is generally poorer. There is little industry, and agriculture is not very productive. Grapes for winemaking and olives are the main crops. To escape poverty, many southern Italians have moved to northern cities, or migrated abroad.

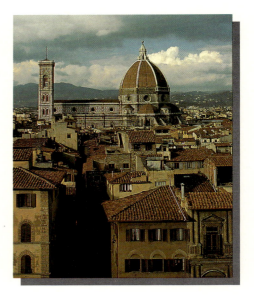

▲ A view across Florence. When it was completed 650 years ago, the dome of the cathedral had the largest span of any building in the world.

▲ Lake Maggiore, on the border between Italy and Switzerland, was carved out by a glacier in the last Ice Age. It is now a popular tourist resort.

Country	Italy	Malta	San Marino	Vatican City
Capital	Rome	Valletta	San Marino	Vatican City
Area (sq km)	301,277	316	61	0.4
Population	57,663,000	354,000	24,000	800
Official language	Italian	Maltese, English	Italian	Latin, Italian

◀ To avoid attack from the mainland, the first Venetians built their homes on small islands in the middle of a sheltered lagoon.

The Balkans and Romania

The Balkans form a giant triangle of land in the southeast corner of Europe. It is a very mountainous region, hot in summer but often bitterly cold in winter. On the mountainsides, sheep and goats are still herded as they have been for thousands of years. Their milk is made into cheese and yoghurt. Great amounts of fruit are grown for export, especially in the fertile valleys of Romania and Bulgaria. Grapes are grown almost everywhere. Most are made into wine, but some are dried to make raisins and sultanas. Olives and olive oil are exported by Greece.

Romania has invested heavily in mines, factories and machinery. Elsewhere there are only small pockets of industry. However, tourism is increasingly popular everywhere, especially along the Mediterranean coastlines of Yugoslavia and Greece and along the Black Sea coasts of Romania and Bulgaria.

All the Balkan countries apart from Greece have been controlled until recently by communist governments. Now things are changing and free elections are being held. In the short term, poverty and unemployment have become widespread. The breakdown of communist rule in Yugoslavia has led to civil war, and the creation of several new countries, including Serbia, Croatia, Bosnia and Slovenia. In Albania, many refugees have attempted to flee to Italy. Despite this, hopes are high that in the longer term each country will be able to restore peace.

▲ About 500 years ago, the eastern shores of the Adriatic Sea were ruled by Venice. This is a Venetian bridge in northern Albania.

▲ Bulgaria has no access to the Aegean Sea, but it is building a huge tourist industry along its sunny Black Sea coastline.

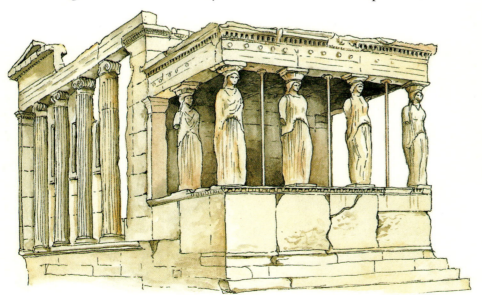

▲ Part of a temple on the Acropolis, or "high city", that overlooks Athens. Most ancient Greek monuments have cylindrical pillars, but here the stone has been carved in the shape of women, called caryatids.

Country	Yugoslavia	Albania	Bulgaria	Greece	Romania
Capital	Belgrade	Tirana	Sofia	Athens	Bucharest
Area (sq km)	255,804	28,748	110,912	131,990	237,500
Population	23,809,000	3,250,000	9,011,000	10,048,000	23,200,000
Official language	Serbo-Croat, Slovene, Macedonian	Albanian	Bulgarian	Greek	Romanian

The Low Countries

Belgium, the Netherlands and Luxembourg are known as the Benelux countries (after their first letters). They are also called the Low Countries, because much of their land is close to sea level.

They are very densely populated, with a long and successful history of agriculture, industry and global trade. Belgium and Luxembourg, for example, have been producing steel and textiles for world markets for well over a century. Brussels, the capital of Belgium, is also the headquarters of the European Community. The Netherlands has hundreds of kilometres of greenhouses producing vegetables and flowers for the whole of Europe.

The Netherlands is often called Holland ("hollow land") because the sea flows right into its centre. For centuries high tides and "superstorms" in the North Sea, as well as river flooding, were a constant danger. But little by little, over hundreds of years, the Dutch have been building high walls called dykes along every coastline and river bank. They can then drain the land back for farming or building. Today, one in four people live on land that was once under water. New land is being created at a rate of about 30 km^2 a year.

▲ *Flags of the member-states fly outside the new European Parliament building in Luxembourg.*

▼ *A village in the wooded hills of the Ardennes, close to the borders of Belgium, Luxembourg and France.*

▲ *Three centuries ago, Amsterdam's land prices were so high that merchants built narrow but extremely tall houses.*

	🇳🇱	🇧🇪	🇱🇺
Country	Netherlands	Belgium	Luxembourg
Capital	Amsterdam & The Hague	Brussels	Luxembourg
Area (sq km)	41,785	30,518	2586
Population	14,943,000	9,845,000	373,000
Official language	Dutch	Flemish (Dutch dialect), French	Letzeburgish (German dialect), French

Scandinavia and Finland

Scandinavia is in the cold northeast of Europe. During the Ice Age, Scandinavia was covered by an ice dome several kilometres thick. As the ice moved, it ground down many of the mountains beneath. It gouged out great valleys, cut deep fiords into the coastline, and created thousands of lakes. When the ice melted, the glaciers and icefields almost disappeared, except for pockets in Norway and Iceland, and coniferous forests grew to cover most of the region.

Vikings once lived in this rugged landscape. They were great sailors and warriors who crossed the Atlantic to colonize Iceland and Greenland. They may even have reached America before Columbus.

Until recently, many Scandinavians lived by fishing for cod and herring. But today, oil and natural gas from the North Sea, and forest products such as timber and paper, have become more profitable. Furniture-making is another great industry for which the region is famous. Dairy and pig farming is important in Denmark, which is generally warmer than the other countries. Sweden, the largest and richest country, has huge deposits of iron ore. It makes many goods out of steel, including cars, guns and cutlery.

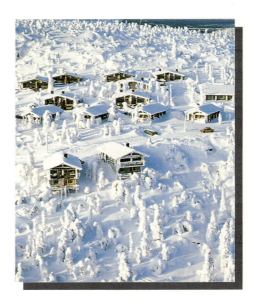

▲ These log cabins, now used only in summer, are on the Arctic Circle, just north of Oulu in Finland.

◄ The deep fiords that bite into Norway's coastline were gouged out by glaciers in the last Ice Age.

▲ A modern North Sea trawler. For centuries Scandinavian sailors have fished the dangerous offshore waters. Some went farther, settling Iceland and Greenland 1000 years ago.

Country	Denmark	Finland	Iceland	Norway	Sweden
Capital	Copenhagen	Helsinki	Reykjavik	Oslo	Stockholm
Area (sq km)	43,092	338,145	103,000	386,975	449,964
Population	5,140,000	4,986,000	255,000	4,242,000	8,559,000
Official language	Danish	Finnish, Swedish	Icelandic	Norwegian	Swedish

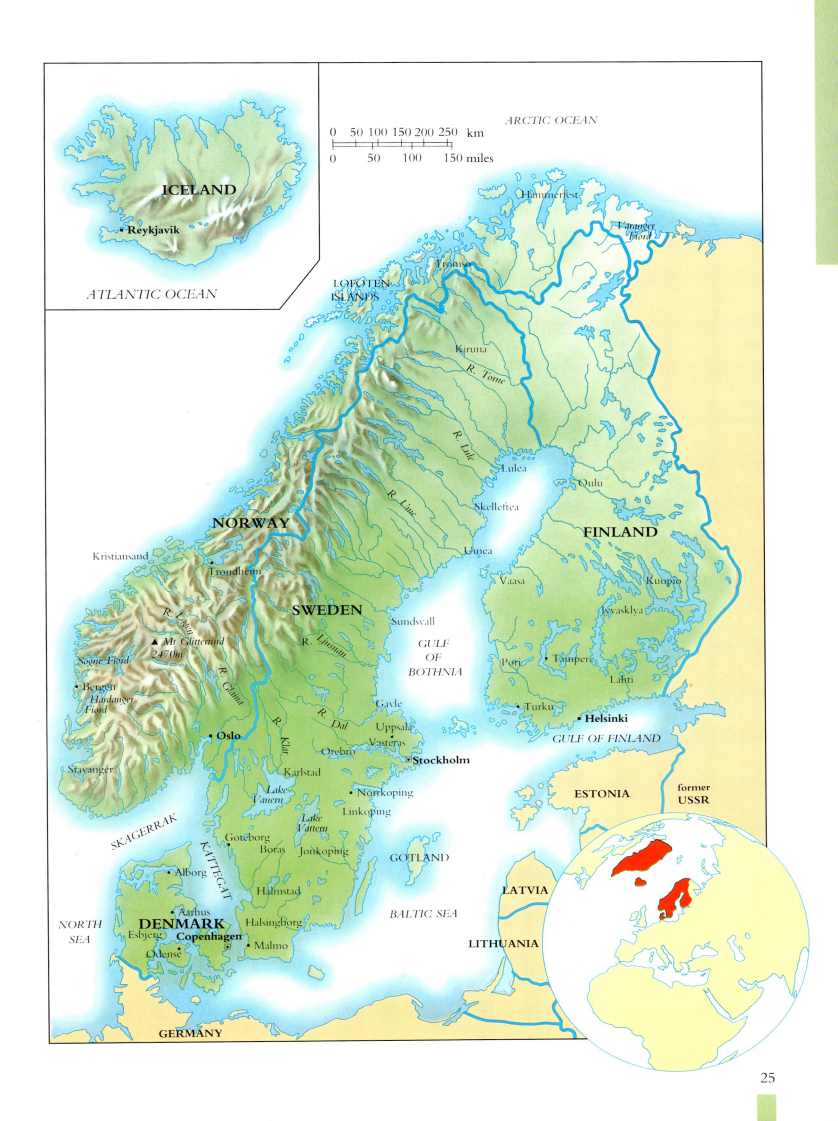

Germany, Switzerland and Austria

Germany, Switzerland and Austria are in the centre of Europe. Most people speak German, though French, Italian and Romansch (a kind of Latin) are spoken in parts of Switzerland.

Much of Austria and Switzerland is covered in mountains known as the Alps. They are famous for their spectacular scenery and sports like climbing and skiing. Many wide, flat-bottomed valleys cut through the Alps, carved out by glaciers in the last Ice Age, over 10,000 years ago. Even when there is snow on the mountain tops, vegetables and fruit can be grown on the sheltered south-facing valley slopes. Fast-flowing mountain rivers are used to produce hydroelectric power. This heats and lights many factories and homes.

Germany is a great industrial nation. The richest area lies in the west, on a huge coalfield in the Ruhr river basin. For the last hundred years, its factories have made everything from guns to textiles. Germany is famous throughout the world for its cars and electrical appliances.

After World War II, Germany was divided east from west by a 900-kilometre wall that snaked south from Lubeck. In 1989, this wall was taken down and the country reunited. But the area that was known as East Germany is now much poorer than West Germany.

▲ Neuschwanstein, a "fairy tale" castle near Munich built for King Ludwig II of Bavaria in the 1800s.

◀ The Swiss city of Geneva lies at the western end of a great lake, where the River Rhône flows into France.

▼ The River Rhine flows from the Swiss Alps past five countries on its 1320-km journey to the North Sea.

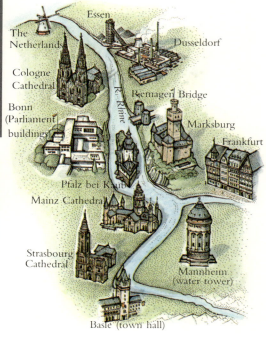

Country	Germany, Federal Republic of	Austria	Liechtenstein	Switzerland
Capital	Berlin	Vienna	Vaduz	Bern
Area (sq km)	357,041	83,855	160	41,293
Population	79,479,000	7,712,000	29,000	6,712,000
Official language	German	German	German	German, French, Italian

Poland, Czechoslovakia and Hungary

Hungary, Poland and Czechoslovakia lie in the centre of Europe, between powerful neighbours. In the past, they have often been invaded and ruled by Germany, Austria or Russia. Today, however, they are independent once again.

Hungary and Czechoslovakia are landlocked. This means they have no sea borders. Poland is so large that some areas are more than 800 km from a port. Luckily, there are many navigable rivers in the region, including the Danube and its tributaries.

Although much of Czechoslovakia is mountainous, most of the rest of the region is flat, or gently rolling. Summers are hot and dry, winters cold and wet. This "continental" climate is perfect for some kinds of agriculture. Poland and Hungary export large amounts of meat, vegetables and fruit, much of it is preserved and canned.

Industry is also important. The coalfields in southeast Poland are Europe's richest. Great shipyards have also been built in port cities such as Gdansk along the Baltic coast. Hungary, though chiefly an agricultural country, also produces iron and steel. One of its biggest and more unusual exports has been the Rubik Cube, which was invented by a Hungarian and exported all over the world.

▲ *Although farming in much of Europe is now highly mechanized, many Polish farmers still use traditional horse-drawn devices.*

Country	Czechoslo-vakia	Hungary	Poland
Capital	Prague	Budapest	Warsaw
Area (sq km)	127,900	93,033	312,683
Population	15,662,000	10,553,000	38,180,000
Official language	Czech, Slovak	Magyar (Hungarian)	Polish

▲ *Hungary's capital Budapest is really two cities, Buda and Pest, separated by the River Danube. Pictured here are the dome and spires of the great Parliament building, built in the last century.*

▶ *Begun more than one thousand years ago, Prague Castle contains a palace and several churches, as well as museums, gardens and schools. It is now the home of Czechoslovakia's president.*

Russia and its Neighbours

Russia, formerly part of the Union of Soviet Socialist Republics (USSR, or Soviet Union) is the world's largest country. It spans Europe and Asia from the Baltic Sea to the Pacific Ocean.

The USSR, which existed until December 1991, was made up of 15 distinct countries, or republics. These were ruled from the capital Moscow by the Communist Party. In 1991 the USSR was dissolved and the Commonwealth of Independent States (CIS) was initially formed by the old republics of Russia, the Ukraine and Byelorussia. The Communist Party was disbanded. The three Baltic states, Estonia, Latvia and Lithuania, declared their independence. Many of the other republics now want to be entirely self-governing.

The major language is Russian, but another 125 languages are spoken. There are also many different religions. In the west of the former USSR, Christianity is the main religion. Muslims are in the majority in the republics bordering on Turkey, Iran and Afghanistan.

The USSR was one of the world's most powerful countries, with a huge army, navy and air force, and a large space industry. It had vast reserves of minerals, including gold, iron, oil and natural gas. It produced immense amounts of grain, cotton and other crops. Yet following the break-up of the USSR, Russia and her neighbours were poor, and the Soviet economy in danger of collapse.

◀ Moscow's walled city, or Kremlin.

▼ A mosque and minaret in Uzbekistan, central Asia. Most people in this region are Muslim.

Country	former USSR (Union of Soviet Socialist Republics)	Estonia	Latvia	Lithuania
Capital	Moscow	Tallinn	Riga	Vilnius
Area (sq km)	16,901,400	45,100	63,700	65,200
Population	140,515,000	1,590,000	2,717,000	3,728,000
Official language	Russian	Estonian	Latvian	Lithuanian

◀ The former Soviet Union encouraged people to maintain their traditional costumes and dances, but not their languages and religions.

The Middle East

Much of the Middle East is barren desert where very few people live. Within the desert are scattered pockets of water called oases, where date palms, vegetables and cereals can be grown. In the past the nomadic Bedouin people used camels, the "ships of the desert", to carry goods between oases and the cities. Now most Bedouin drive trucks instead.

Crops can also be grown on the narrow coastal strip and in many of the valleys within the mountains of Lebanon, Turkey and Iran. In the past, one of the most fertile places on Earth was Mesopotamia, the land between the rivers Tigris and Euphrates. Today, many areas in Israel and Jordan have been reclaimed from the desert by modern methods of irrigation, and now produce abundant crops.

There have been many wars in this region. Three world religions grew up and have their holiest places here: Christianity, Judaism, and Islam. Today, most middle eastern people are Muslims, except in Israel where the majority are Jews. There are also many Christians, especially in Lebanon and Cyprus. Wars have been fought between the different religious groups.

The Middle East is a very wealthy region because of its oil. Most of the world's known oilfields are found under the desert here. Pipelines carry the oil to the Persian Gulf or the Mediterranean Sea where it is pumped into huge tankers for transport round the world.

▲ *For centuries people in Oman's desert have used irrigation canals to water their date palms and other crops.*

▼ *Persepolis, Iran, an awesome relic of a great civilization destroyed by Alexander the Great in 330 BC.*

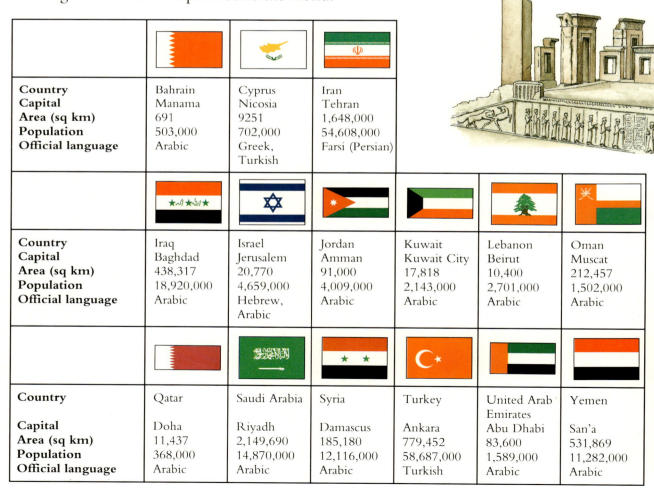

Country Capital Area (sq km) Population Official language	Bahrain Manama 691 503,000 Arabic	Cyprus Nicosia 9251 702,000 Greek, Turkish	Iran Tehran 1,648,000 54,608,000 Farsi (Persian)			
Country Capital Area (sq km) Population Official language	Iraq Baghdad 438,317 18,920,000 Arabic	Israel Jerusalem 20,770 4,659,000 Hebrew, Arabic	Jordan Amman 91,000 4,009,000 Arabic	Kuwait Kuwait City 17,818 2,143,000 Arabic	Lebanon Beirut 10,400 2,701,000 Arabic	Oman Muscat 212,457 1,502,000 Arabic
Country Capital Area (sq km) Population Official language	Qatar Doha 11,437 368,000 Arabic	Saudi Arabia Riyadh 2,149,690 14,870,000 Arabic	Syria Damascus 185,180 12,116,000 Arabic	Turkey Ankara 779,452 58,687,000 Turkish	United Arab Emirates Abu Dhabi 83,600 1,589,000 Arabic	Yemen San'a 531,869 11,282,000 Arabic

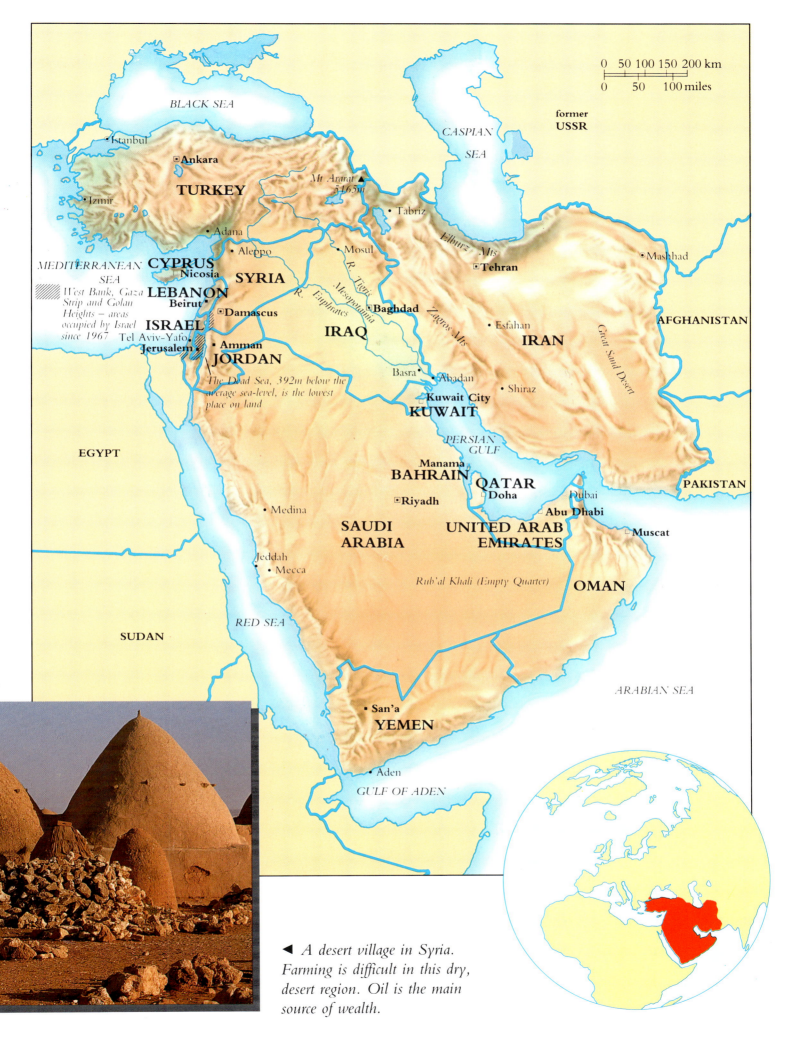

◀ A desert village in Syria. Farming is difficult in this dry, desert region. Oil is the main source of wealth.

India and its Neighbours

India and its neighbours are sometimes known as South Asia. The population of this region is spread unevenly. Very few live in the mountains and deserts of the far north. Yet the nearby plains on either side of the River Indus and the River Ganges are so fertile that they are some of the world's most densely-populated areas.

Most of the people live in villages and farm the land but food is often in short supply. Most families have only small plots of land, and not enough money to buy machinery or fertilizers. Many areas are very dry and rely on the annual monsoon, a brief period of rain that occurs in summer.

Many people leave the land to try to get jobs in the cities. Most are forced to live in overcrowded conditions and have poorly paid jobs. But India and Pakistan in particular have made great strides in recent years, and both countries have many large industries.

The region is deeply divided by religion and language – India alone has 854 dialects. Most Indians are Hindus. The majority in Sri Lanka, Bhutan and Nepal are Buddhists. Elsewhere, most people are Muslims.

▲ *A small boy in Pakistan studies Islam's sacred book, the Koran.*

◄ *A Himalayan scene in northern India. These snowy summits are 6500m high.*

	🇧🇩	🇳🇵	🇵🇰	🇱🇰
Country	Bangladesh	Nepal	Pakistan	Sri Lanka
Capital	Dhaka	Kathmandu	Islamabad	Colombo
Area (sq km)	143,998	147,181	879,902	64,652
Population	115,594,000	18,916,000	112,050,000	16,993,000
Official language	Bengali	Nepali	Urdu	Sinhala
	🇧🇹	🇮🇳	🇲🇻	🇦🇫
Country	Bhutan	India	Maldives	Afghanistan
Capital	Thimphu	New Delhi	Malé	Kabul
Area (sq km)	46,500	3,203,975	298	652,225
Population	1,517,000	827,057,000	215,000	16,121,000
Official language	Dzongkha, Nepali, English	Hindi, English	Divehi (a form of Sinhalese)	Pashtu, Farsi (Persian)

▲ *A Mogul temple and palace at Jaisalmer, a city that lies in the desert of northern India.*

▲ The tiger, once common in India, is now rare and protected.

35

China and its Neighbours

China has the largest population in the world. Much of the west and north of China is barren desert and mountain. East of Manchuria lies the Korean Peninsula. Since 1950, Korea has been divided into two countries, a communist North and a capitalist South.

Most people in China live in the east, along the river valleys and the coastline. Rice is the most important crop in the hot, wet south. In the colder north, wheat and barley are grown. In the extreme north is Mongolia, a desert area where few people live. Since 1949 China has been a communist country. Many factories have been set up, and its vast mineral resources such as iron ore, coal and oil are mined. Although progress has been made, the country is still poor and faces many problems.

Tibet is a mountain plateau so high that it has been called "the roof of the world". Several great rivers such as the Yangtze and the Mekong have their source in these mountains.

Hong Kong and Macao are Chinese ports that have been ruled by European powers for more than a century. By agreement between China, Britain and Portugal, in 1997 both will be returned to China.

▲ Old and new in Hong Kong's magnificent natural harbour. Traditional boats called junks still carry goods, but Hong Kong's wealth is now based on its modern "high-tech" industries and banks.

Country	Macau	China	Hong Kong	Mongolia	North Korea	South Korea	Taiwan
Capital	Macau	Beijing (Peking)	Hong Kong	Ulan Bator	Pyongyang	Seoul	Taipei
Area (sq km)	17	9,556,100	1072	1,565,000	120,538	99,016	36,002
Population	479,000	1,139,060,000	5,801,000	2,190,000	21,773,000	42,793,000	20,345,000
Official language	Portuguese Cantonese (Chinese)	Mandarin (Chinese)	Cantonese (Chinese) English	Mongolian	Korean	Korean	Mandarin

▶ Sichuan, China's most populous area, consumes immense amounts of rice. With a warm, wet climate, up to three crops can be grown a year.

Japan

Japan is a group of islands off the coast of East Asia. It consists of four main islands and about 3000 smaller ones. The landscape is mountainous with little room for farming. Japan has a large population for its size.

Most Japanese live in the south, where the climate is warmer. They eat mostly rice, fish and vegetables. Most Japanese are very healthy, living longer on average than the people of any other nation. Men expect to live to be 74, women to 80.

Japan is the richest country in the world, after the United States, in spite of having hardly any minerals and having to import its raw materials. But Japan is wealthy because of its efficient factories. Japan leads the world in the use of robots, and its high quality goods are in great demand. Japan's chief exports are "high-tech" goods like video cameras, CD players and cars. Japan is not only one of the world's most powerful economies but also a leading trading nation. It exports nearly £160 billion worth of goods each year.

One in four of Japan's population live in and around Tokyo, the world's largest city. Tokyo has the best earthquake-proof buildings in the world. This is hardly surprising because the city sometimes suffers from several earthquakes every day. Most of the quakes are small, but the occasional larger one can cause havoc. The worst earthquake this century happened in 1923, when the whole of Tokyo was destroyed and more than 100,000 people died.

Country	Japan
Capital	Tokyo
Area (sq km)	377,801
Population	123,537,000
Official language	Japanese

▲ *A Japanese shrine. Most people in Japan have two religions, Buddhism and ancestor-worship or Shinto.*

▶ *A farm worker in northern Honshu. Every bit of agricultural land is intensively farmed.*

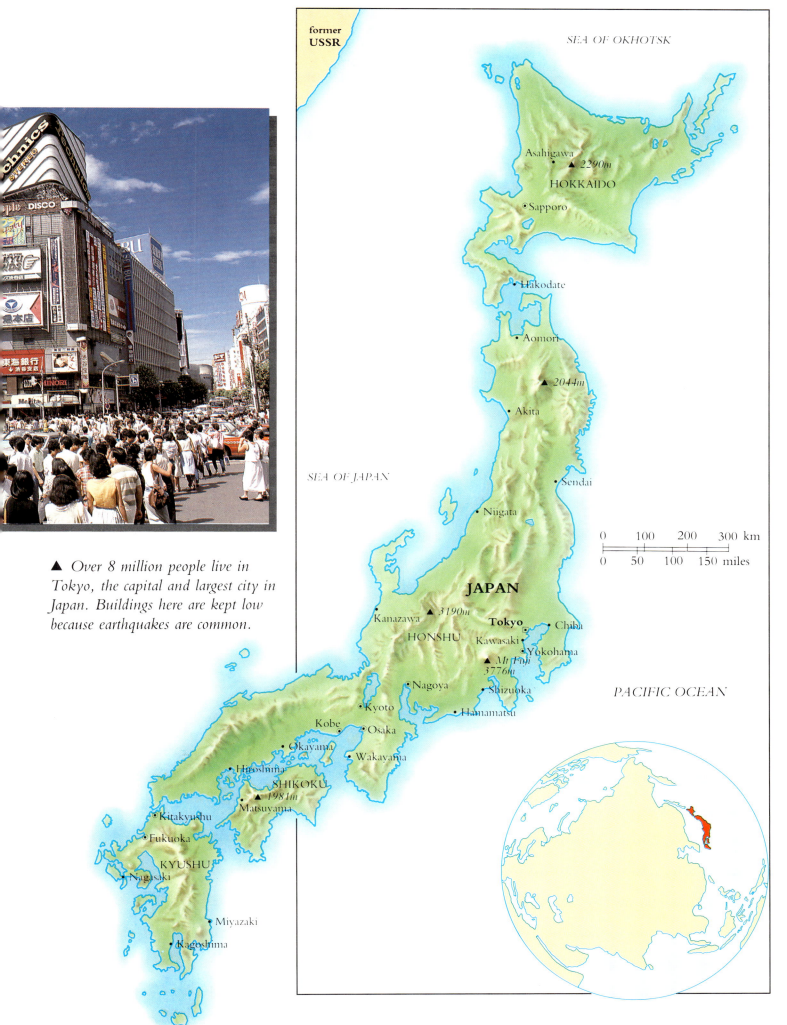

▲ Over 8 million people live in Tokyo, the capital and largest city in Japan. Buildings here are kept low because earthquakes are common.

39

Southeast Asia

Southeast Asia is one of the world's most densely-populated regions. It has such a hot, wet climate that much of it was once covered in "jungle", now called tropical rainforest. Today, many of the most valuable trees have been cut down. In their place are huge plantations where crops such as pineapples, sweet corn, rubber, tea or tobacco are grown for export.

Indonesia is a republic lying along an archipelago of about 13,500 islands, including the island of Java, one of the most densely populated areas of the world. The Dutch became the chief European traders in Southeast Asia in the 1700s. Singapore, one of the world's largest ports and international banking centres, lies off the tip of the Malayan Peninsula. It was a British colony for over a hundred years. Today this small "city-state" is an independent republic.

Rice grows well in Southeast Asia. Two or even three crops can be grown each year. Fields are cut into the sides of the steep hills to form paddies that rise like steps. Low earth dikes hold the water. Water is made to drain slowly from field to field. Fish can also be reared in the drowned fields. Ducks and pigs are allowed to roam freely.

Minerals are also important. Malaysia mines much of the world's tin, and Indonesia and the tiny state of Brunei produce great amounts of oil. Industry is increasing everywhere. New factories have sprung up in most countries to make cars, or "high-tech" goods such as computers, televisions and other electronic equipment.

Many religions are practised in this area. Most of the people on the mainland are Buddhists. The majority throughout Indonesia are Muslims, though the people of Bali are chiefly Hindu.

▲ A village in Sulawesi, part of Indonesia. The saddle-shaped roofs help to repel the rain.

▲ A floating market in Bangkok. Tradition survives here, but Thailand is also one of the world's fastest-growing economies.

Country	Cambodia	Indonesia	Myanmar (Burma)	Brunei
Capital	Phnom Penh	Jakarta	Rangoon	Bandar Seri Begawan
Area (sq km)	181,035	1,919,443	676,557	5765
Population	8,246,000	179,300,000	41,675,000	266,000
Official language	Khmer	Bahasa (Indonesian)	Burmese	Malay

Country	Philippines	Singapore	Thailand	Vietnam	Malaysia
Capital	Manila	Singapore	Bangkok	Hanoi	Kuala Lumpur
Area (sq km)	300,000	636	513,115	329,556	334,758
Population	61,480,000	3,003,000	57,196,000	66,200,000	17,861,000
Official language	Pilipino, English	Malay, Chinese, Tamil, English	Thai	Vietnamese	Malay

Canada

Canada is the world's second-largest country, after Russia. A train journey across country from the Atlantic to the Pacific oceans takes at least four days and five nights. Canada's coastline includes 58,500 km of mainland and 185,000 km of islands. But Canada has a relatively small population because of its climate and landscape.

In the far north, summer is short. For most of the year the land is covered in ice and snow. Only hunters, mineral prospectors and a few tourists venture into this frozen landscape. Oil and gas have recently been discovered here. Farther south, forestry is the main industry. Canada is one of the world's chief producers of paper.

Across central Canada are flat, fertile prairies where the winters are freezing and the summers are very hot. Wheat is grown here in such huge fields that you can travel for many kilometres without seeing a boundary fence. Canada produces so much wheat it is often called the "breadbasket" of the world.

Today, most Canadians live in cities close to the border with the United States, particularly around the Great Lakes and the St Lawrence Seaway. Canada was settled by the French in the 1600s and later by the British who took over the colony. Because of this, Canada today has two official languages, English and French. Most French-speakers live in Quebec. Elsewhere most people speak English. Many people in Quebec want to be independent from the rest of the country.

Country	Canada
Capital	Ottawa
Area (sq km)	9,970,610
Population	26,522,000
Official languages	English, French

▲ Bow Lake, Alberta. The Rockies are part of a mountain chain that runs from Alaska to Mexico.

▶ The city of Vancouver, British Columbia, on Canada's western coastline, is thriving thanks to trade across the Pacific.

▶ The hotel Château Frontenac, a landmark of the city of Quebec. The city was founded by Samuel de Champlain, a French explorer, in 1608. Most of the people in this part of Canada are French-speaking.

The United States

The United States is the world's richest and most powerful country. Almost every kind of environment can be found here. There are great snow-capped mountain ranges, flat prairie grasslands, swamps, hot deserts and evergreen forests. The nation can grow most of its own food crops, and many minerals can be found somewhere on its territory. But it has so many people and industries that it has to import many raw materials, such as iron ore and tin, from other parts of the world.

The United States is a republic formed by the union of 50 states. The first 13 states were formed from the original colonies that broke away from Britain in 1776. Hawaii, a group of islands 4700 km out in the middle of the Pacific Ocean, became the 50th state in 1959.

Most US citizens have ancestors who emigrated from Asia, Africa or Europe in the last 250 years. American Indians have lived in North America for more than 20,000 years. Many towns, rivers and other natural features bear Indian names. Mississippi, for example, meant "Great River" in the Algonquian Indian language.

Today English is the common language of the entire United States, but many places such as Los Angeles, California and New Orleans, Louisiana, still have the names given to them by the the first Spanish, French, Dutch or other European settlers.

◀ *Autumn comes to Waits River, Vermont. Autumn in New England brings a tapestry of bright colours to the landscape.*

▼ *Most US ranches are on the dry grasslands between Montana in the north and Texas in the south.*

Country	United States of America
Capital	Washington, D.C.
Area (sq km)	9,529,202
Population	249,975,000
Official language	English

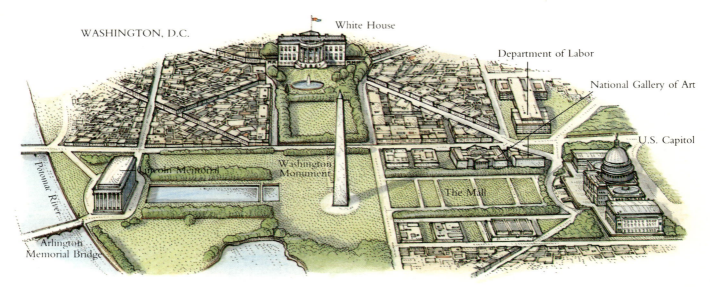

▲ The US capital, Washington D.C., is named after the first US president, George Washington. Its grand layout was planned about 200 years ago by a French engineer, Pierre Charles L'Enfant, who was commissioned by Washington. The White House is the president's official home.

▲ The skyline of Dallas, Texas is lit up by the dying sun. Only the city centre is tall, but the surrounding districts sprawl for miles.

◀ Snow-capped Mount Rainier, in the state of Washington, was once a fiery volcano more than 4000m high. Now wildflowers carpet its sides.

◀ Until recently, American football was played mainly in the USA. Now it is spreading to other countries. Soccer, probably the world's most widely-played sport, is rapidly becoming popular in the USA, too.

STATE	POPULATION (1990)	BIRD	FLOWER	TREE
Alabama	4,040,587	Yellowhammer	Camellia	Southern pine
Alaska	550,043	Willow ptarmigan	Forget-me-not	Sitka spruce
Arizona	3,665,228	Cactus wren	Saguaro	Paloverde
Arkansas	2,350,725	Mockingbird	Apple blossom	Pine
California	29,760,021	California valley quail	Golden poppy	California redwood
Colorado	3,294,349	Lark bunting	Rocky Mt. columbine	Blue spruce
Connecticut	3,287,116	Robin	Mountain laurel	White oak
Delaware	666,168	Blue hen chicken	Peach blossom	American holly
Florida	12,937,926	Mockingbird	Orange blossom	Cabbage palm
Georgia	6,478,216	Brown thrasher	Cherokee rose	Live oak
Hawaii	1,108,229	Néné	Hibiscus	Kukui
Idaho	1,006,749	Mountain bluebird	Syringa	White pine
Illinois	11,430,602	Cardinal	Violet	White oak
Indiana	5,544,159	Cardinal	Peony	Tulip tree
Iowa	2,776,755	Eastern goldfinch	Wild rose	Oak
Kansas	2,477,574	Western meadowlark	Sunflower	Cottonwood
Kentucky	3,685,296	Cardinal	Goldenrod	Kentucky coffee tree
Louisiana	4,219,973	Brown pelican	Magnolia	Bald cypress
Maine	1,227,928	Chickadee	White pine cone and tassel	Eastern white pine
Maryland	4,781,468	Baltimore oriole	Black-eyed Susan	White oak
Massachusetts	6,016,425	Chickadee	Mayflower	American elm
Michigan	9,295,297	Robin	Apple blossom	White pine
Minnesota	4,375,099	Common loon	Pink and white lady's slipper	Norway pine
Mississippi	2,573,216	Mockingbird	Magnolia	Magnolia tree
Missouri	5,117,073	Bluebird	Flowering dogwood	Hawthorn
Montana	799,065	Western meadowlark	Bitterroot	Ponderosa pine
Nebraska	1,578,385	Western meadowlark	Goldenrod	Cottonwood
Nevada	1,201,833	Mountain bluebird	Sagebrush	Single-leaf piñon
New Hampshire	1,109,252	Purple finch	Purple lilac	White birch
New Jersey	7,730,188	Eastern goldfinch	Violet	Red oak
New Mexico	1,515,069	Roadrunner	Yucca	Piñon
New York	17,990,455	Bluebird	Rose	Sugar maple
North Carolina	6,628,637	Cardinal	Flowering dogwood	Pine
North Dakota	638,800	Western meadowlark	Wild prairie rose	American elm
Ohio	10,847,115	Cardinal	Scarlet carnation	Buckeye
Oklahoma	3,145,585	Scissor-tailed flycatcher	Mistletoe	Redbud
Oregon	2,842,321	Western meadowlark	Oregon grape	Douglas fir
Pennsylvania	11,881,643	Ruffed grouse	Mountain laurel	Hemlock
Rhode Island	1,003,464	Rhode Island Red	Violet	Red maple
South Carolina	3,486,703	Carolina wren	Carolina jessamine	Palmetto
South Dakota	696,004	Ring-necked pheasant	American pasqueflower	Black Hills spruce
Tennessee	4,877,185	Mockingbird	Iris	Tulip poplar
Texas	16,986,510	Mockingbird	Bluebonnet	Pecan
Utah	1,722,850	Seagull	Sego lily	Blue spruce
Vermont	562,758	Hermit thrush	Red clover	Sugar maple
Virginia	6,187,358	Cardinal	Flowering dogwood	Dogwood
Washington	4,866,692	Goldfinch	Coast rhododendron	Western hemlock
West Virginia	1,793,477	Cardinal	Rhododendron	Sugar maple
Wisconsin	4,891,769	Robin	Violet	Sugar maple
Wyoming	453,588	Western meadowlark	Indian paintbrush	Cottonwood

Mexico, Central America & the Caribbean

Central America is like a bridge and the Caribbean like stepping stones between North and South America. The Panama Canal, which is 82 km long, cuts across the mainland at its narrowest point. Mexico is part of North America; Central America includes all those countries between Mexico and Colombia in South America. When Europeans first arrived, about 500 years ago, they were amazed by the civilization of the Aztec people of central Mexico. The Aztec capital, where Mexico City is today, was larger than any capital in Europe at the time.

In much of Mexico the land is very dry and barren, but farther south the region is heavily forested. Much of the forest is being burnt or cut down to make way for plantations. Sugar cane, coffee, bananas and tobacco are the most common crops. Land is now being planted with grass to feed cattle. There are many minerals in the area, including aluminium and oil. But there is still very little manufacturing industry.

Most of the people now living in Central America and the Caribbean are of American Indian or African descent. There are also many whose ancestors came from Europe.

Country	Belize	Nicaragua	Panama	St Kitts and Nevis	St Lucia	St Vincent and the Grenadines	Trinidad and Tobago
Capital	Belmopan	Managua	Panama City	Basseterre	Castries	Kingstown	Port of Spain
Area (sq km)	22,963	130,000	77,082	269	616	388	5128
Population	188,000	3,871,000	2,418,000	44,000	151,000	116,000	1,227,000
Official language	English, Spanish	Spanish	Spanish, English	English	English	English	English
Country	Dominican Republic	El Salvador	Guatemala	Haiti	Honduras	Jamaica	Mexico
Capital	Santo Domingo	San Salvador	Guatemala City	Port-au-Prince	Tegucigalpa	Kingston	Mexico City
Area (sq km)	48,442	21,041	108,889	27,750	112,088	10,991	1,958,201
Population	7,170,000	5,252,000	9,197,000	6,486,000	5,105,000	2,420,000	86,154,000
Official language	Spanish	Spanish	Spanish	French	Spanish	English	Spanish
Country	Antigua & Barbuda	Bahamas	Barbados	Grenada	Costa Rica	Cuba	Dominica
Capital	St John's	Nassau	Bridgetown	St George's	San José	Havana	Roseau
Area (sq km)	443	13,934	430	344	51,100	110,861	790
Population	77,000	253,000	255,000	85,000	2,994,000	10,609,000	83,000
Official language	English	English	English	English	Spanish	Spanish	English

◄ An Easter procession in Guatemala. The majority of people in Central and South America are Roman Catholic Christians.

◄ Samana, in the Dominican Republic.

► Chichen Itza, Yucatan Peninsula, Mexico. Maya Indians built a city here 1000 years ago.

The Andean Countries

The Andes is one of the world's greatest mountain ranges, running for about 8000 km down the entire west coast of South America. There are many volcanoes along its length.

The equator passes through Ecuador, as you might guess from its name. Many lowland areas in Ecuador and its neighbour Colombia are hot and wet, ideal conditions for bananas and sugar cane. The cooler slopes of the mountains are chiefly devoted to coffee growing. Many of the rivers that feed the Amazon rise in the Andes. As they flow eastward to the Amazon basin, they pass through thick, tropical rainforest.

Rainfall is heavy on the eastern slopes of the Andes. But the top of the mountains and the Pacific coastline are very dry. In some years, Peru's capital, Lima, receives no rain at all. The high mountain plateaus can also be very cold, and there is little vegetation.

Before the Europeans arrived in the 1500s, the Inca people ruled a vast empire. But millions of them were wiped out by diseases like measles, smallpox and influenza brought over by Spanish settlers.

Many plants now grown throughout the world originated in the Andes – for example potatoes and tomatoes. At first Europeans were reluctant to eat these strange new foods, but eventually they became accepted almost everywhere.

▲ *The Inca city of Machu Picchu, Peru, was never discovered by the Spanish invaders.*

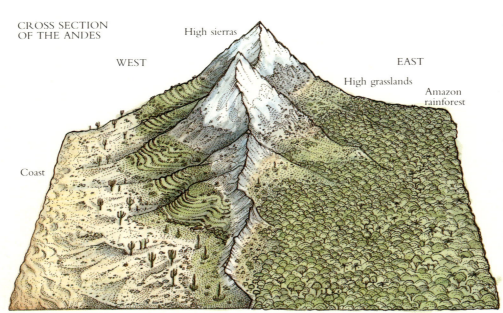

◀ *The Andes mountains run like a spine down the length of South America. In this region, the eastern side (right) is wet and heavily forested. The west is very dry.*

▼ *The nimble guanaco is the wild ancestor of the llama and alpaca.*

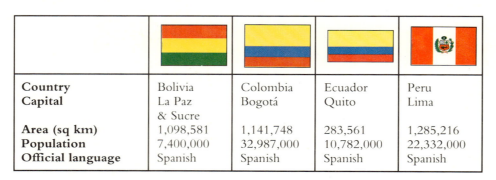

	Bolivia	Colombia	Ecuador	Peru
Country	Bolivia	Colombia	Ecuador	Peru
Capital	La Paz & Sucre	Bogotá	Quito	Lima
Area (sq km)	1,098,581	1,141,748	283,561	1,285,216
Population	7,400,000	32,987,000	10,782,000	22,332,000
Official language	Spanish	Spanish	Spanish	Spanish

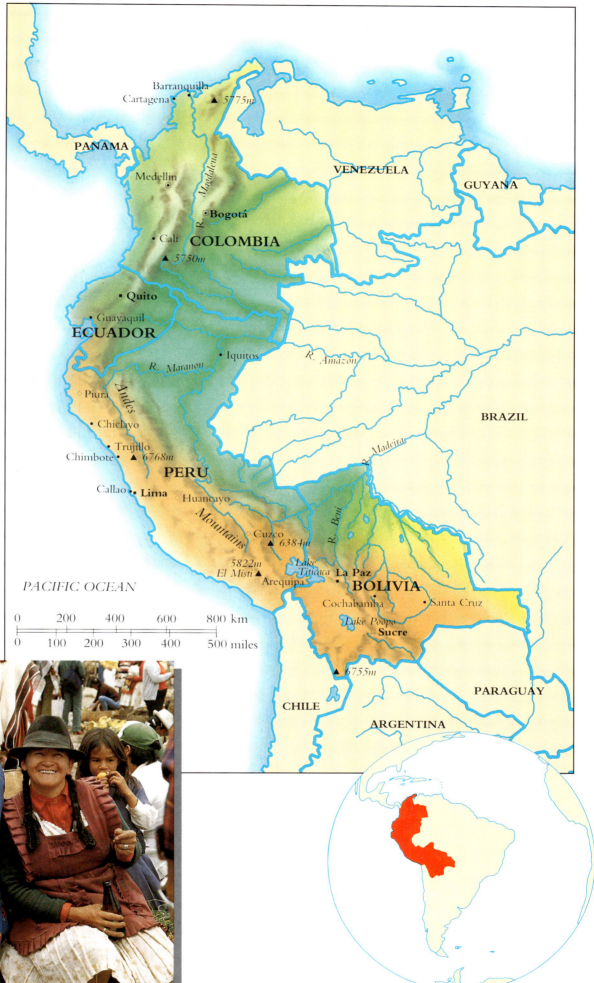

▼ Small markets such as this one in Colombia can be found throughout the Andes. People trek many miles to buy and sell and meet friends.

51

Brazil and its Neighbours

The Amazon, the world's second-longest river, flows across this vast region, the widest part of South America. Large ships can travel upstream as far as Iquitos, 3200 km from the sea. Most of the land is covered in thick, hot and very wet rainforest. Very few people live here, apart from small groups of Indians. They grow crops in small fields, fish in the rivers, and hunt and gather food from the forest.

Many millions of people have settled in the region from almost every part of Europe, Africa and Asia. Most countries in Central and South America are now Spanish-speaking. Brazil is an exception. The majority of people here speak Portuguese. In three small countries in the northeast, other European languages are spoken: English in Guyana, Dutch in Surinam, and French in French Guiana.

In the past, rubber, coffee, sugar and beef have been Brazil's most important products. Now, almost everybody lives in cities on the coast, such as São Paulo and Rio de Janeiro, where there are many modern industries. But there is also a great deal of poverty, as poor farmers from the countryside move to the cities, looking for work.

To the northwest of Brazil is Venezuela. It has a large oil industry, and rich deposits of iron ore.

▲ Beneath the floor of Venezuela's Lake Maracaibo is one of the world's richest oilfields.

Country	Venezuela	Brazil	French Guiana (France)	Guyana	Surinam
Capital	Caracas	Brasilia	Cayenne	Georgetown	Paramaribo
Area (sq km)	912,050	8,511,965	91,000	214,969	163,820
Population	19,735,000	150,368,000	99,000	796,000	422,000
Official language	Spanish	Portuguese	French	English	Dutch, English

▲ Brasilia, Brazil's ultra-modern capital. Until 1960, the capital was Rio de Janeiro, on the coast. By moving 800 km inland, the government hoped more settlers would move into the forested interior.

▶ Rainforests have many distinct layers between the ground and the tree canopy up to 50m above it. Each has quite different animals and plants. Today the rainforests are under threat as thousands of hectares are felled to harvest valuable hardwoods or to create farmland.

Argentina and its Neighbours

Cattle and sheep far outnumber people in Argentina, Uruguay and the inland nation of Paraguay. Huge areas of these countries are covered in rich grasslands. The herds and flocks are tended by cowboys called gauchos. A large amount of wheat is also grown. Most food is exported – the meat is canned, or transported in refrigerated ships. These countries also have many industries, including steel, cars and textiles.

The border between Argentina and Chile runs along the top of the Andes. This means that Chile has a very odd shape. It is more than 3000 km long, but in places less than 50 km wide. In the north, the Atacama Desert is one of the driest places on Earth. One part of the desert had no rain for 400 years.

Central Chile is very fertile. Vegetables and fruits are grown there for export to Europe, Asia and North America. Its location in the southern hemisphere gives Chile an advantage. Fruit is ripening in Chile's summer when it is mid-winter in the northern hemisphere.

In the far south, conditions are very cold, windy and foggy. The frozen wastes of Antarctica are only 1300 km away. Thousands of ships have been destroyed trying to pass through the stormy Strait of Magellan or round Cape Horn.

▲ *Great herds of cattle, driven by cowboys called* gauchos, *can be found throughout this region. Much of the beef is exported to Europe.*

▲ *Bleak and icy Patagonia, in the far south of Argentina and Chile, is so cold that some of its glaciers flow into the sea.*

Country	Argentina	Chile	Paraguay	Uruguay
Capital	Buenos Aires	Santiago	Asunción	Montevideo
Area (sq km)	2,780,092	756,626	406,752	177,414
Population	32,322,000	13,173,000	4,277,000	3,094,000
Official language	Spanish	Spanish	Spanish	Spanish

◀ The Congress Building in Buenos Aires, capital and largest city in Argentina. The name Buenos Aires is Spanish for the "good winds" sailors needed for their journey across the Atlantic Ocean to Europe or round Cape Horn.

North Africa

The Sahara is by far the largest, hottest desert in the world. It has less than 25 cm of rainfall a year and covers over 7,700,000 square km, nearly one quarter of all Africa. The highest temperature ever recorded was 58°C in the shade, in a village in Libya. Most of the desert is a rocky plateau. Very little is sandy, and there are few oases. Across the south of the region is a very dry area known as the Sahel.

For centuries people have crossed the Sahara on camels, the "ships of the desert". They traded goods such as gold, salt and spices. The "caravans" of camels took weeks to cross from the Mediterranean to places like Timbuktu. Today, it is easier to use lorries or planes, and there are roads that run from Algeria to Niger.

Most of the very best agricultural land lies around the Mediterranean coast, in oases and beside rivers. The River Nile floods every year. The fertile Nile Valley made Egypt one of the richest of the ancient civilizations. Today, the Aswan Dam controls the floodwaters and generates electricity.

▶ *The Nile flows north through Sudan and Egypt into the Mediterranean Sea.*

						NO FLAG AVAILABLE
Country **Capital** **Area (sq km)** **Population** **Official language**	Algeria Algiers 2,381,741 24,960,000 Arabic	Morocco Rabat 446,550 25,061,000 Arabic	Niger Niamey 1,267,000 7,732,000 French	Sudan Khartoum 2,505,813 25,204,000 Arabic	Tunisia Tunis 163,610 8,180,000 Arabic	Western Sahara Laayonne 66,000 179,000 Arabic, Berber, Spanish
Country **Capital** **Area (sq km)** **Population** **Official language**	Chad N'Djamena 1,284,000 5,679,000 French	Egypt Cairo 1,001,449 53,153,000 Arabic	Ethiopia Addis Ababa 1,251,282 49,241,000 Amharic	Libya Tripoli 1,759,540 4,545,000 Arabic	Mali Bamako 1,240,000 8,156,000 French	Mauritania Nouakchott 1,025,520 2,025,000 Arabic, French

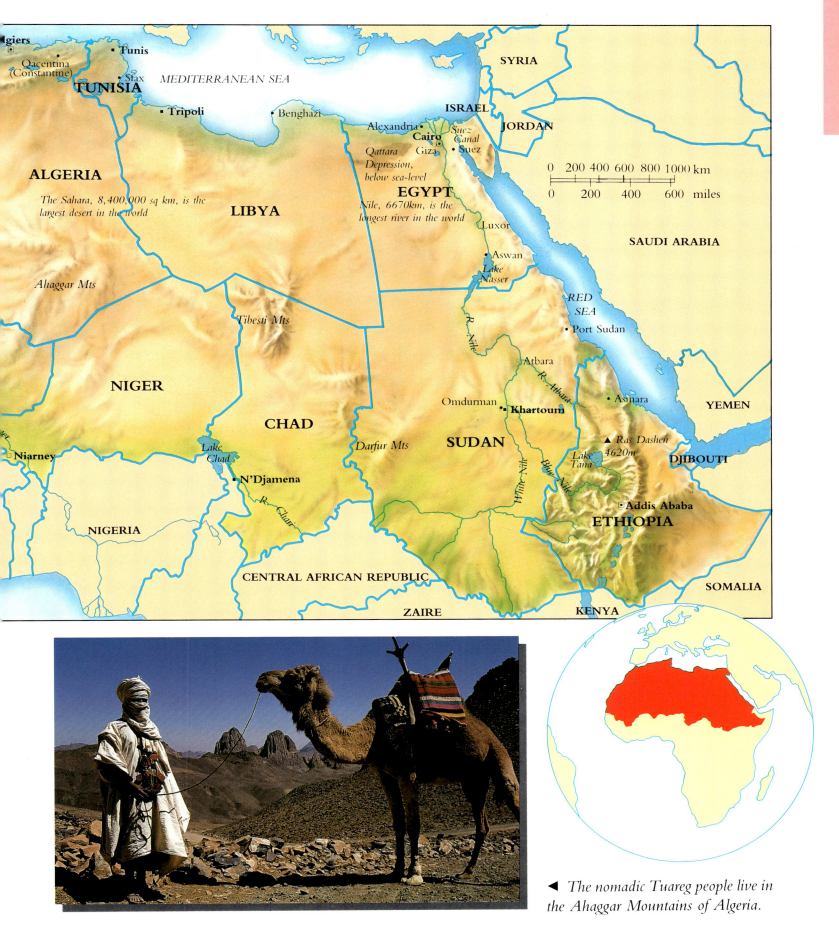

◀ The nomadic Tuareg people live in the Ahaggar Mountains of Algeria.

West Africa

Many of the countries of West Africa are long and narrow, with short coastlines. Their capital cities are generally located on the coast. Many of them grew as ports for the slave trade. These countries were later ruled as colonies by Britain, France or Portugal. This explains why their official languages may be English, French or Portuguese.

There are also thousands of different African languages spoken in West Africa. A single country may have many different languages and peoples. This has sometimes caused conflict between peoples, especially in Nigeria, where there are more than 250 different groups.

Most of the region is hot and wet, because it lies close to the Equator. Dense rainforest used to cover most of the land, but much of this has now been cut down for timber and farmland. There are plantations, growing such crops as cocoa, coffee, and rubber for export. Great numbers of cattle, kept for their meat, milk and hides, are grazed in the drier grassland areas in the north.

Although farming is the main occupation in these countries, there are many modern cities where new industries have started. There are also many mineral-rich areas. Diamonds are mined in Sierra Leone, and gold in Ghana. Oil is Nigeria's most important export. Tourism is increasingly important in countries such as Gambia.

▼ Four hundred years ago, the Benin people made beautiful objects out of ivory, wood and bronze. They lived south of the River Niger.

Country	Senegal	Sierra Leone	Togo
Capital	Dakar	Freetown	Lomé
Area (sq km)	196,722	72,325	56,785
Population	7,327,000	4,151,000	3,531,000
Official language	French	English	French

Country	Equatorial Guinea	Benin	Guinea-Bissau	Cote d'Ivoire (Ivory Coast)	Liberia	Nigeria	São Tomé and Principe
Capital	Malabo	Porto Novo	Bissau	Abidjan	Monrovia	Lagos	São Tomé
Area (sq km)	28,051	112,600	36,125	322,500	99,067	923,768	964
Population	348,000	4,736,000	965,000	11,998,000	2,607,000	108,542,000	121,000
Official language	Spanish	French	Portuguese	French	English	English	Portuguese

Country	Cameroon	Congo	Gabon	Gambia	Ghana	Guinea	Burkina Faso
Capital	Yaoundé	Brazzaville	Libreville	Banjul	Accra	Conakry	Ouagadougou
Area (sq km)	475,442	342,000	267,667	11,295	238,533	245,857	274,200
Population	11,834,000	2,271,000	1,172,000	861,000	15,028,000	5,756,000	9,001,000
Official language	English, French	French	French	English	English	French	French

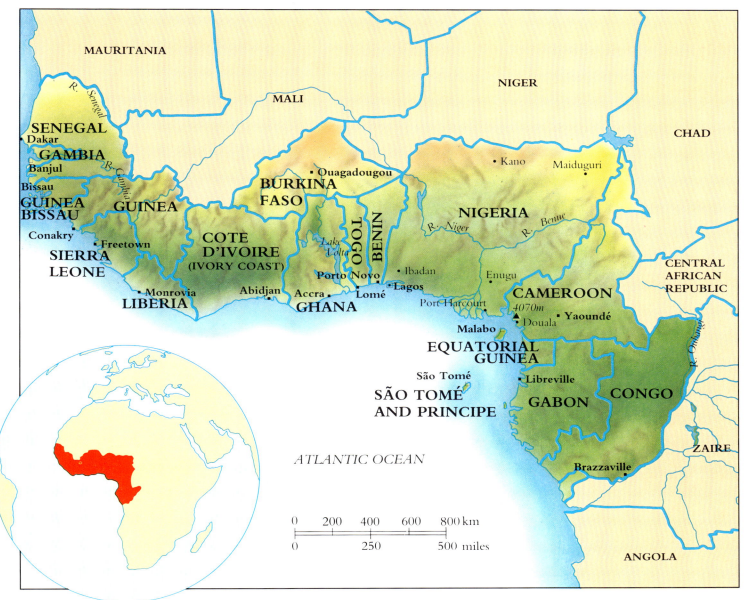

▼ Modern dams such as this one across the River Volta in Ghana are important sources of electricity in West Africa.

▶ Crafts flourish in Africa's growing cities. This man is printing batik cloth in Gambia's capital, Banjul.

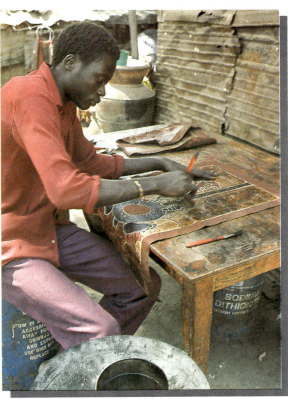

Central and East Africa

The majority of Africans in Central Africa live close to Lake Victoria, near the borders between Kenya, Uganda and Tanzania. In the past, Europeans settled in this area, growing tea, coffee, cotton and sisal. Most people farm the land, but diamonds are mined in Tanzania, and Uganda exports huge amounts of copper. In Kenya and Tanzania, tourism is a major business. Many people come here to see wild animals roaming freely in the great national parks.

In the drier parts of the region, people are nomadic. They move about in a constant search for grass for their herds of cattle to eat. This often leads to fights with farmers whose land they wander on to. Conditions can be most severe for people in Somalia and eastern Ethiopia. This region is called the "Horn of Africa" after its horn-like shape that sticks out into the Indian Ocean. Serious famines, causing much starvation, have become very common here.

To the west is the enormous Zaire (Congo) River. Most of the land it passes through is dense rainforest, which is hot and very wet. Zaire's forests contain many valuable hardwoods, such as ebony and mahogany. Zaire is the world's leading producer of industrial diamonds and exports copper and uranium ore. The southern grasslands have national parks full of wildlife. Zaire is almost completely landlocked. Notice how short its coastline is in comparison with its huge size.

▲ A woman of the Samburu people of northern Kenya, lavishly dressed in ceremonial jewellery. Like many people of this region, the Samburu live by herding cattle.

Country	Central African Republic	Djibouti	Somalia
Capital	Bangui	Djibouti	Mogadishu
Area (sq km)	622,984	23,200	6,327,657
Population	3,039,000	409,000	7,497,000
Official language	French	French	Somali
Country	Burundi	Uganda	Zaire
Capital	Bujumbura	Kampala	Kinshasa
Area (sq km)	27,830	241,139	2,345,095
Population	5,458,000	18,795,000	35,562,000
Official language	French, Kirundi	English	French
Country	Rwanda	Kenya	Tanzania
Capital	Kigali	Nairobi	Dodoma
Area (sq km)	26,338	582,646	945,087
Population	7,181,000	24,032,000	25,635,000
Official language	French, Kinyarwanda	English, Swahili	English, Swahili

▲ Kenya's modern capital city, Nairobi, is 1700m above sea level. But Kenya lies on the Equator, so it is very warm.

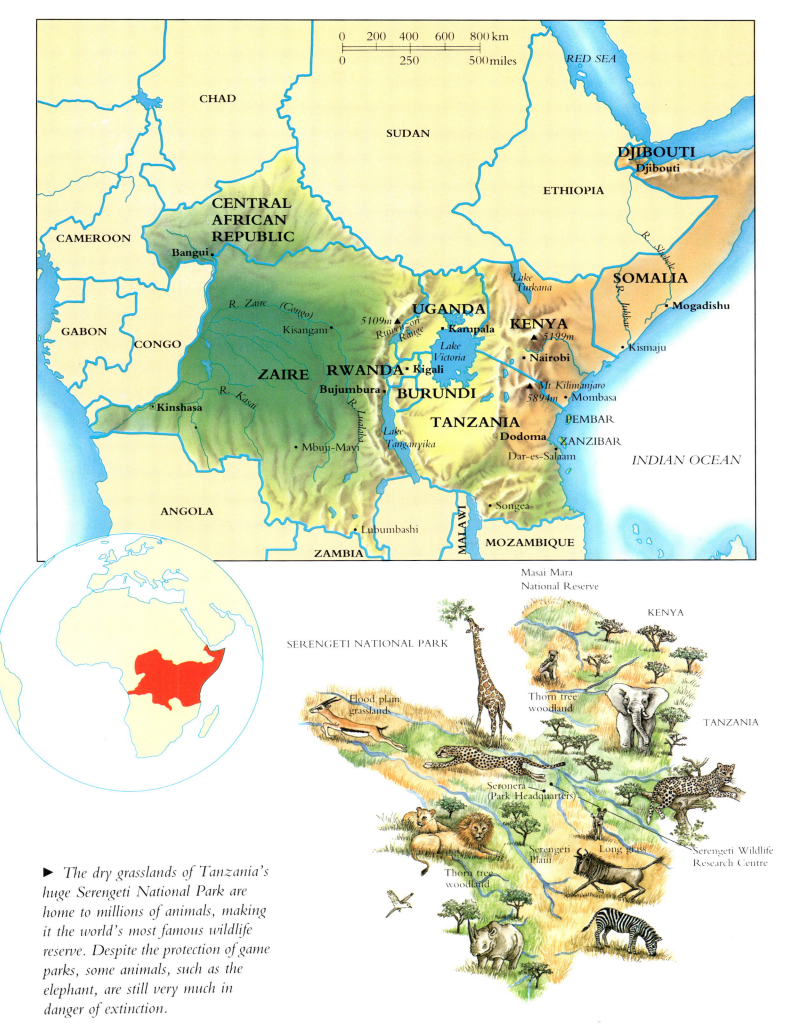

▶ The dry grasslands of Tanzania's huge Serengeti National Park are home to millions of animals, making it the world's most famous wildlife reserve. Despite the protection of game parks, some animals, such as the elephant, are still very much in danger of extinction.

Southern Africa

Southern Africa has two great deserts, the Namib and the Kalahari. It almost never rains in the Namib. The Kalahari is less bleak. The Khoi-San (Bushmen) who live here know their desert so well they can find food and water almost anywhere.

Many of the southern African countries have rich mineral deposits such as diamonds, copper and uranium, and fertile land. Until recently, all have been ruled by European countries, or by white minority governments. Now, they are independent.

The most powerful and richest country in the region is South Africa. It has the largest population, many of whose ancestors came from Europe and southern Asia. Today, the two main languages they speak are English and Afrikaans, a kind of Dutch. For much of this century the white South African government has had a policy called *apartheid*. This meant that whites and non-whites were kept apart. Non-whites were not allowed to vote and did not have the same opportunities in such things as education, jobs or places to live. Now apartheid is being ended.

▲ Known to the world as Victoria Falls, the local name means "the Smoke that Thunders" because clouds of spray are hurled 500m into the air.

◀ Deep underground, a miner drills for gold in a mine near Johannesburg, South Africa. South Africa is the world's largest producer of gold, a precious natural resource.

Country	Angola	Botswana	Comoros	Lesotho	Madagascar	Malawi
Capital	Luanda	Gaborone	Moroni	Maseru	Antananarivo	Lilongwe
Area (sq km)	1,246,700	582,000	2235	30,355	587,041	118,484
Population	10,020,000	1,291,000	551,000	1,774,000	11,197,000	8,289,000
Official language	Portuguese	English, Setswana	French	English, Sesotho	French, Malagasy	English, Chichewa
Country	Namibia	South Africa,	Swaziland	Zambia	Zimbabwe	Seychelles
Capital	Windhoek	Pretoria, Cape Town & Bloemfontein	Mbabane & Lobamba	Lusaka	Harare	Victoria
Area (sq km)	823,144	1,123,226	17,364	752,614	390,759	453
Population	1,781,000	35,282,000	768,000	8,073,000	9,369,000	67,000
Official language	Afrikaans, English	Afrikaans, English	English	English	English	English, French

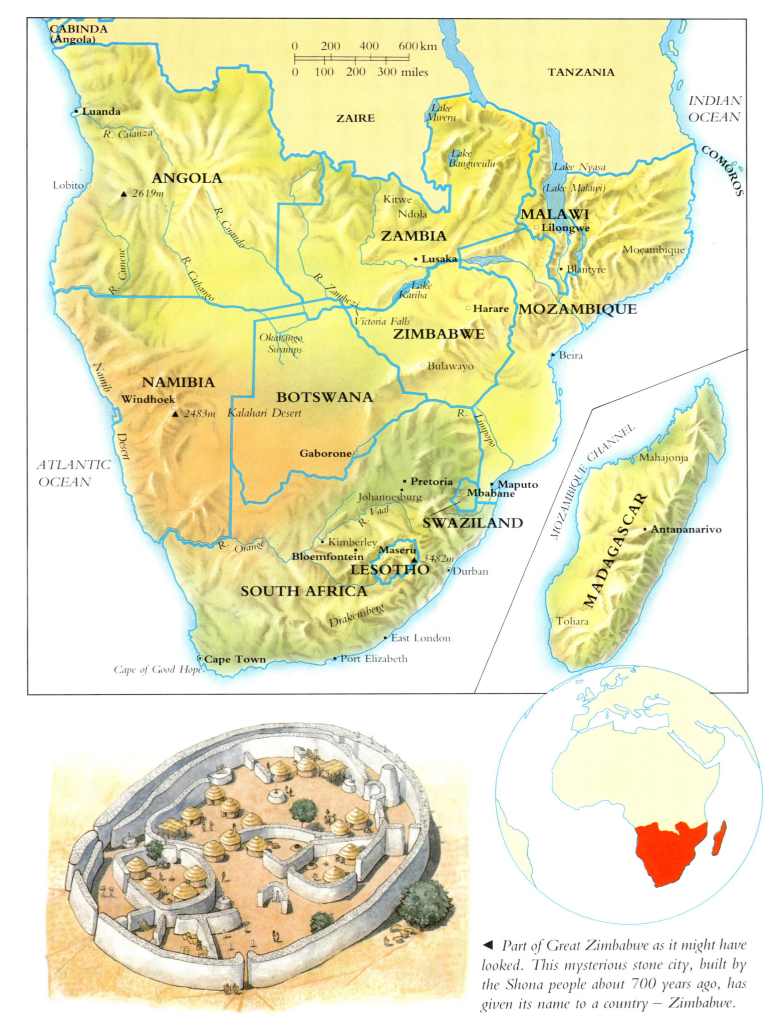

◀ Part of Great Zimbabwe as it might have looked. This mysterious stone city, built by the Shona people about 700 years ago, has given its name to a country – Zimbabwe.

Australia

Australia is a rich and varied land. It has great potential for mining, farming and industry. The best land for farming is around the coast in the extreme southeast and southwest, and between the Great Dividing Range and the coast.

Much of the east of the country is dry grassland or "Outback". This is suitable for grazing Australia's millions of sheep and cattle provided they have plenty of space to wander. It rarely rains, but wells have been dug to supply the animals with water.

There is some tropical rainforest in the north of the country where logging is an important industry. In the dry centre and west are large areas of desert. But the area has become rich thanks to its abundant minerals, including coal, copper, iron, lead and uranium.

The first European settlers arrived in 1788. Most were convicts, sent "Down Under" from the British Isles. Before them, people called Aborigines (which means "here from the start") lived in Australia. Since 1950, many immigrants have come from other parts of Europe, Asia and the Pacific islands. Today, Australia has more people living in cities than any other country. Most of these cities are on the coast.

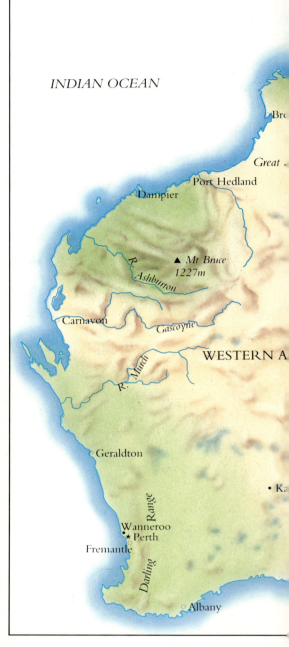

Country	Australia
Capital	Canberra
Area (sq km)	7,682,300
Population	17,086,000
Official language	English

▲ Sydney, Australia's largest and most spectacular city, is built around a magnificent natural harbour.

▶ Aborigines were Australia's first inhabitants. This young man has painted his face in traditional style.

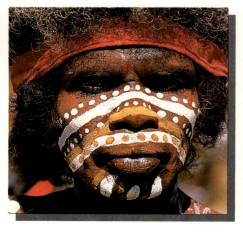

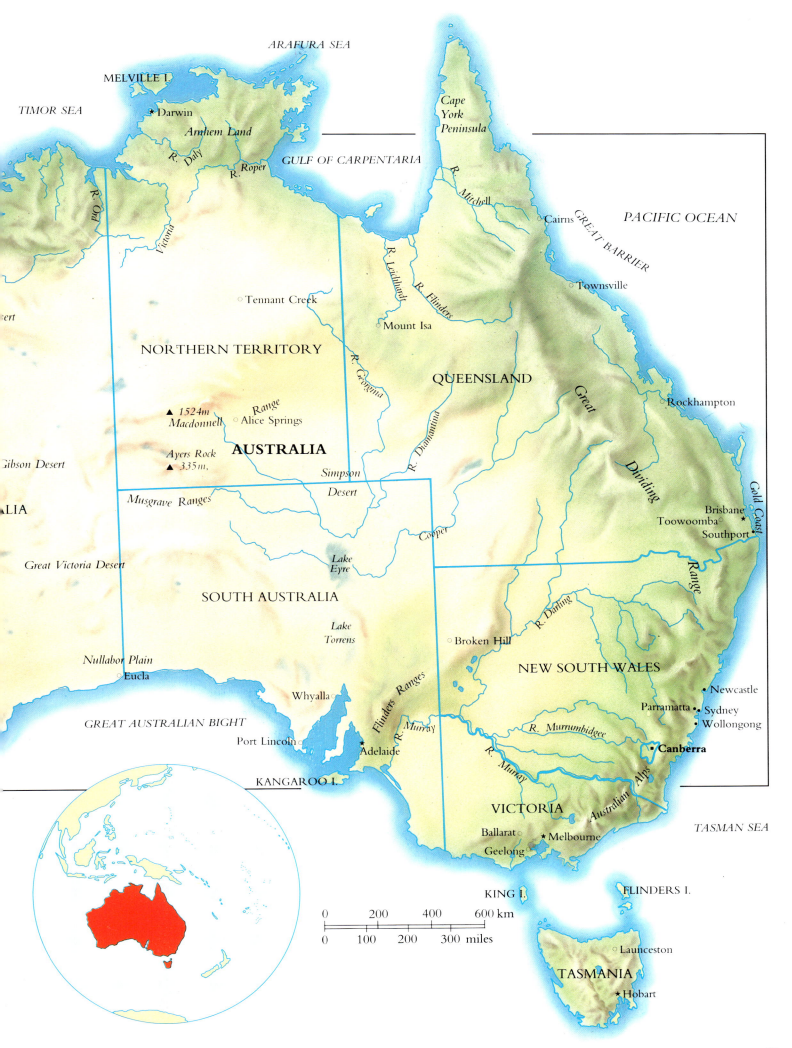

New Zealand and the Pacific

The Pacific Ocean covers nearly half the globe. There are immense distances between the thousands of tiny islands that are dotted throughout. Many are inhabited. The people live by fishing, or growing crops in tiny fields. There are some foreign-owned plantations, producing cocoa, coffee and other crops for export.

New Zealand is made up of two major islands. The South Island is cool and mountainous. Three-quarters of the people live on the warmer North Island. Farming is New Zealand's main source of wealth. Sheep and cattle outnumber people 20 times over. Sheep are grazed mainly in the south. In the north, a great dairy industry produces cheese and butter for export. A large variety of vegetables and fruits are grown, including the kiwi fruit, which is exported all over the world.

Most New Zealanders are of European ancestry, and English is the most widely-spoken language. The people who inhabited the country before Europeans arrived are Maoris. Many Maoris were killed by early settlers, but recently they have increased in numbers again and are demanding the return of their lands.

▲ *Rainbow lorikeet, Papua New Guinea.*

▼ *(Left) Wellington, New Zealand, is one of the world's windiest cities; small earthquakes occur almost daily.*

Country	Tonga	Fiji	New Zealand
Capital	Nuku'alofa	Suva	Wellington
Area (sq km)	750	18,333	268,112
Population	95,000	765,000	3,346,000
Official language	English	English, Fijian	English

Country	Tuvalu	Vanuatu	Western Samoa	Kiribati	Nauru	Papua New Guinea	Solomon Islands
Capital	Funafuti	Port-Vila	Apia	Tarawa	Nauru	Port Moresby	Honiara
Area (sq km)	26	12,189	2831	726	21	462,840	28,370
Population	10,000	147,000	164,000	66,000	10,000	3,699,000	321,000
Official language	English, Tuvalu	Bislama, English, French	English, Samoan	English, Gilbertese	English, Nauruan	English	English

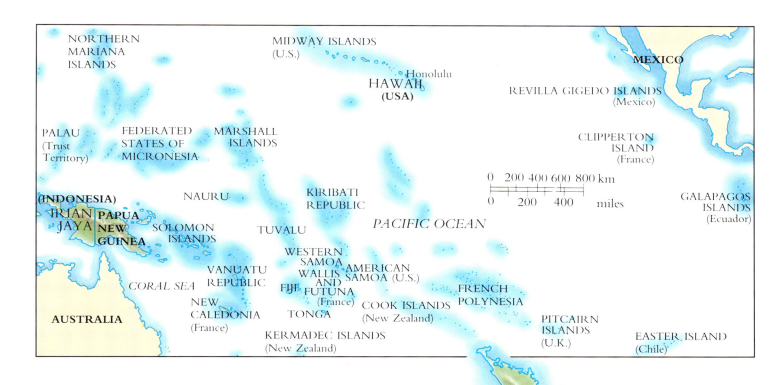

▲ Nobody knows who made these giant figures on Easter Island, or why. There are 600 of them, some as large as 20m high. They were carved over 1000 years ago. The builders may have died out before their work was completed.

The Polar Lands

ARCTIC

The Arctic is not a continent. Unlike the Antarctic, there is no land underneath the frozen ocean. Indeed, submarines have passed right under the North Pole. The ice cap grows during the northern winter, and gets smaller during the summer.

Nobody lives on the ice cap, except in a few scientific research stations. But people live round it, in the countries that are close to the Arctic Circle. Some, such as the Inuit (Eskimos) of North America and Greenland and the Aleuts of the Aleutian Islands live by fishing and hunting seals, whales and other animals. The Lapps of Scandinavia and the Chukchi of northern Siberia keep herds of reindeer. Recently, people have started to extract oil, gas and coal from a number of places inside the Arctic Circle.

Polar bear

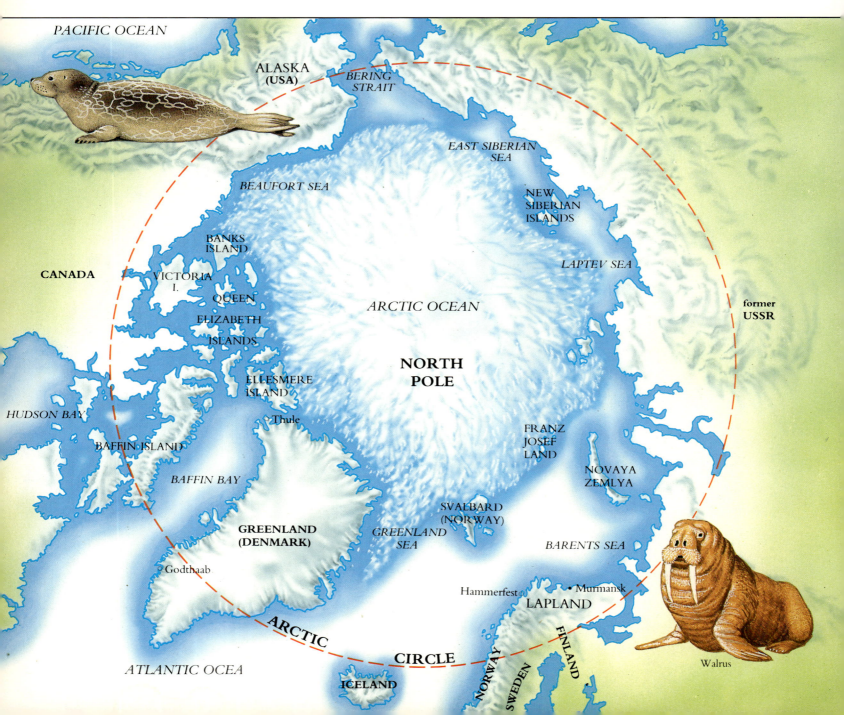

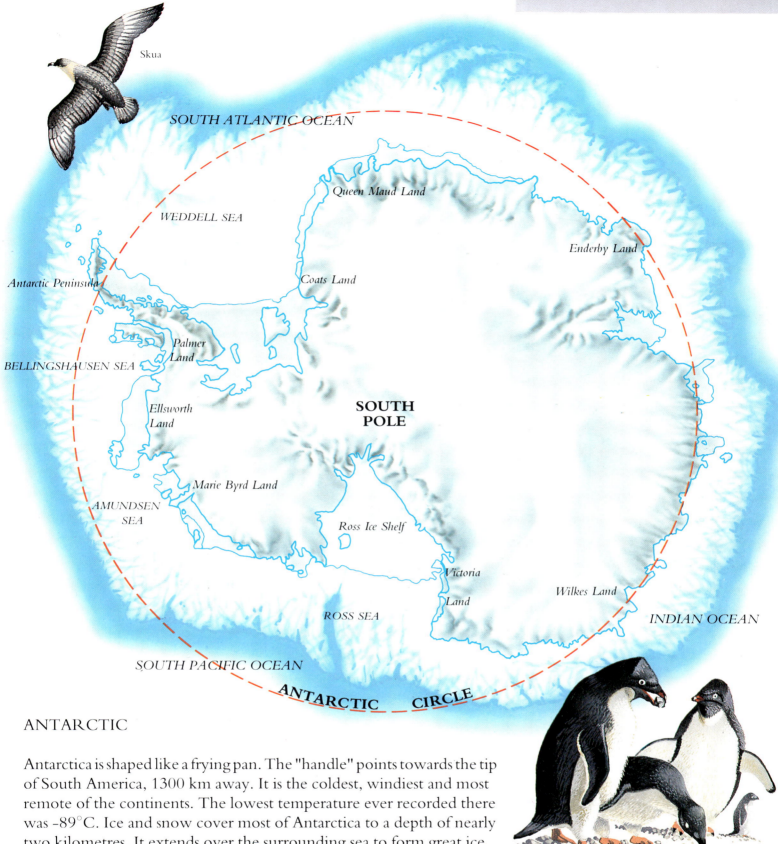

Adelie penguins

ANTARCTIC

Antarctica is shaped like a frying pan. The "handle" points towards the tip of South America, 1300 km away. It is the coldest, windiest and most remote of the continents. The lowest temperature ever recorded there was -89°C. Ice and snow cover most of Antarctica to a depth of nearly two kilometres. It extends over the surrounding sea to form great ice shelves hundreds of metres thick. From time to time icebergs as big as whole countries break off and float away into the ocean. They break up and melt as they travel northwards.

Few animals and plants live in Antarctica, but the surrounding seas are rich in wildlife, including fish, whales, birds, seals and small shrimp-like creatures called krill.

Even at the height of summer (which is winter in the northern hemisphere), there are only 4000 people on the whole continent. They are mostly scientists, working in research stations.

Many countries claim rights over wedges of Antarctica. But it has been agreed that no country should be allowed to "own" it.

The Earth: *Facts and Figures*

EARTH FACTS

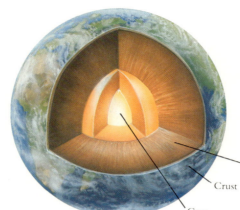

Circumference round the Equator: 40,075 kilometres.

Circumference round the Poles: 40,007 kilometres.

Distance to centre of Earth: about 6370 kilometres.

Surface area: about 510,065,600 square kilometres; the Earth is farther away from the Sun in July than in January.

Rotation Speed: at the Equator, the Earth rotates on its axis at 1660 kilometres per hour.

Speed in orbit: The Earth travels at 29.8 kilometres per second.

Average distance from Moon: 385,000 kilometres.

▲ *Rolling dunes in the Moroccan Sahara. This great desert covers most of North Africa.*

LARGEST ISLANDS
	square kilometres
Greenland	2,175,600
New Guinea	794,090
Borneo	751,078
Madagascar	587,041
Baffin I.	476,066
Sumatra	431,982
Honshu	230,822
Great Britain	229,522
Ellesmere	198,393
Victoria I.	192,695

OCEANS
	square kilometres
Pacific	181,000,000
Atlantic	106,000,000
Indian	73,490,000
Arctic	14,350,000

HIGHEST MOUNTAINS
	metres
Everest (Himalaya-Nepal/Tibet)	8848
Godwin Austen (Pakistan/India)	8607
Kanchenjunga (Himalaya-Nepal/Sikkim)	8597
Makalu (Himalaya-Nepal/Tibet)	8470
Dhaulagiri (Himalaya-Nepal)	8172
Nanga Parbat (Himalaya-India)	8126
Annapurna (Himalaya-Nepal)	8075
Communism Peak (Pamir-former USSR)	7495
Aconcagua (Andes-Argentina)	6960
McKinley (Alaska-USA)	6194
Kilimanjaro (Tanzania)	5895

MAJOR WATERFALLS
Highest	metres
Angel Falls (Venezuela)	979
Tugela Falls (South Africa)	948
Yosemite Falls (California)	739

Greatest Volume	cubic metres per second
Niagara (N.America)	6,000

LARGEST LAKES
	square kilometres
Caspian Sea (former USSR/Iran)	438,695
Superior (USA/Canada)	82,409
Victoria Nyanza (Africa)	69,484
Aral (former USSR)	67,770
Huron (USA/Canada)	59,570
Michigan (USA)	58,016
Baikal (former USSR)	34,180
Tanganyika (Africa)	31,999
Great Bear (Canada)	31,598
Malawi* (Africa)	28,490

*Also called Lake Nyasa

LONGEST RIVERS
	kilometres
Nile (Africa)	6670
Amazon (S.America)	6437
Mississippi-Missouri-Red Rock (N.America)	6231
Yenisei (former USSR)	5540
Chang Jiang (Yangtze) (China)	5470
Ob-Irtysh (former USSR)	5150
Zaire* (Africa)	4828
Lena (former USSR)	4828
Amur (Asia)	4506
Huang He (China)	4345
Mackenzie-Peace (Canada)	4240
Lanchang Jiang (SE Asia)	4184

*Formerly Congo River

DESERTS
	square kilometres
Sahara	8,400,000
Australian Desert	1,550,000
Arabian Desert	1,300,000
Gobi	1,040,000
Kalahari	520,000

▼ *The summit of Mt Everest. The peak towers above the photographer, who took the picture at 5500m.*

General Index

Page numbers in *italics* refer to captions to illustrations

Aborigines 64, *64*
Adriatic Sea 20
Afrikaans language 62
Alcantara *17*
Aleutian Islands 68
Algarve 16
Alps 14, 18, 26
Aluminium 48
Amazon basin 50, 52
Amsterdam 22
Andes Mts 50, *50*, 54
Apartheid 62
Apennines 18
Arctic Circle *24*
Ardennes Mts 22
Aswan Dam 56
Atacama Desert 54
Athens 20
Automobiles *see* Motor vehicle industries
Aztec civilization 48
Bananas 48, 50
Bangkok *40-1*
Banjul *59*
Barcelona *16*
Barley 36
Bedouin people 32
Beef 52
Benin people *58*
Ben Nevis *12*
Black Sea coast *20-1*
Brasilia 52
Brussels 22
Budapest *28*
Buddhism 34, 36, 38, 40
Buenos Aires *54-5*
Camels 56
Cape Horn 54
Caribbean 48
Cattle 12, 48, 54, *54-5*, 58, 64, 66
Chang Jiang (Yangtze) river 36
Cheeses 14, 20, 66
Chichen Itza *49*
Christianity 18, 30, 32, *49*
Chukchi people 68
Clothing 18, *60*
Coal 12, 26, 28, 36, 64, 68
Cocoa 58, 66
Coffee 48, 50, 52, 58, 60, 66
Commonwealth of Independent States (CIS) 30
Communism 20, 30, 36
"Continental" climate 28
Copper 60, 62, 64
Costa Blanca/del Sol 16
Cotton 30, 60
Crafts *59*
Dairy farming 12, 14, 20, 24, 66
Dallas 46
Dams 56, *59*
Dance *31*
Danube river 28
Date palms 32
Deserts 32, *32-3*, 34, 36, 44, 54, 56, 62, 64, 70, *70*
Diamonds 58, 60, 62
Diseases 50
Dutch language 52
Dutch settlers/traders 40, 44

Dykes 22
Earth facts 70
Earthquakes 18, 38, 66
Easter Island 66-7
Emigration 18, 34, 44, 64
English language 42, 44, 52, 58, 62, 66
Equator 50, *60*
European Community 22, *22*
Everest, Mt *70*
Famine 56, *60*
Financial services 12, 40
Fiords 24, *24*
Fish/fishing 16, 24, *24*, 38, 40, 52, 66, 68
Florence *18*
Flowers 22
Forests/forestry 12, 24, 42, 44, 48, *50* *see also* Rainforests, tropical
French language 26, 42, 44, 52, 58
Fruit 12, 20, 26, 28, 40, 54, 66
Furniture-making 24
Ganges river 34
Gauchos 54, *54-5*
Gdansk 28
Geneva 26
German language 26
Gibraltar 16
Glaciers 24, *24*, 26, 54
Goats 20
Gold 30, 56, 58, *62*
Grains 12, 30, 36, 42, 54
Grasslands 42, 44, *44*, 54, 58, 60, 64
Great Dividing Range 64
Great Lakes 42
Greenhouses 22
Hardwoods 60
Herculaneum 18
Herding 20, 56, 60, *60*, 68
High technology industries 12, 38, 40
Himalayas 34
Hindus 34
Hong Kong 36
Honshu 38
Horses *28-9*
Hunters 42, 52
Hydroelectricity 18, 26, 56, *59*
Icebergs 69
Inca civilization 50, *50-1*
Indians, American 44, 48, 52
Indus river 34
Inuit (Eskimo) people 68
Iquitos 52
Iron 16, 24, 28, 30, 36, 44, 52, 64
Irrigation 32, *32*, 40
Islam 16, 30, 32, 34, *34*, 40
Islands, largest 70
Italian language 26
Jaisalmer *34-5*
Jerez 16
Judaism 32
Jura Mts 14
Kalahari Desert 62
Khoi-San (Bushmen) 62
Kiwi fruit 66
Lakes, largest 10, 11, 70
Lanchang Jiang (Mekong) river 36
Lapp people 68
Lead 64
Lima 50
Logging 64
London *12*
Luxembourg 22

Lyon 14
Machu Picchu *50-1*
Magellan, Strait of 54
Maggiore, Lake *18*
Maori people 66
Maracaibo, Lake 52
Markets *40-1, 51*
Mayan civilization *49*
Meat products 28, 52, 54
Mediterranean Sea 32
Mineral prospectors 42
Mining 12, 20, 36, 40, 62, 64
Mississippi river 44
Monaco 14
Monsoon rains 34
Moscow *30*
Motor vehicle industries 14, 16, 18, 24, 26, 38, 54
Mountains, highest 10, 11, 70
Music *31*
Muslims *see* Islam
Nairobi 60
Namib Desert 62
Natural gas 24, 30, 42, 68
Neuschwanstein Castle *26*
New England 44
Nile river 56, *56*
Nomadic peoples 32, *57*, 60
North Sea 12, 24, *24*
Nuclear power 14
Oases 32, 56
Oceans 70
Oil *12*, 24, 30, 32, 36, 40, 42, 48, 52, *52*, 58, 68
Olives 16, 18, 20
Oporto 16
Panama Canal 48
Paper production 24, 42
Paris 14, *14*
Patagonia *54*
Persepolis *32*
Persian Gulf 32
Pig farming 24, 40
Pompeii 18
Po river valley 18
Portuguese language 52, 58
Potatoes 50
Prague *29*
Prairies 42, 44, *44*
Pyrenees 14
Quebec 42, *43*
Rainforests, tropical 40, 50, 52, *53*, 58, 60, 64 *see also* Forests/forestry
Rainier, Mount *46*
Raisins 20
Reclamation of land 22, 32
Refugees 20
Reindeer 68
Rhine river 14, *26*
Rhone river 14, *26*
Rice 36, *37*, 38, 40
Rio de Janeiro 52, *52*
Rivers, longest 10, 11, 70
Robots 38
Rocky Mts 42
Roman Catholic Church 18, *49*
Romans, Ancient *12*, *17*
Romansch language 26
Rome 18
Rubber 40, 52, 58
Ruhr river basin 26
Russian language 30

Sahara Desert 56, 70
Sahel 56
St Lawrence Seaway 42
Salt 56
Samana (Dominican Republic) *49*
Samburu people *60*
Sao Paulo 52
Seine river 14, *14*
Serengeti National Park *61*
Sheep 12, 20, 54, 64, 66
Shintoism 38
Shipbuilding 12, 28
Sichuan 36
Sintra *16*
Sisal 60
Slave trade 58
Space industries 30
Spanish language 44, 52
Spanish settlers 50
Spices 56
Sports 26, *46*
Steel 16, 22, 24, 28, 54
Strasbourg 14
Sugar 48, 50, 52
Sulawesi 40
Sultanas 20
Swamps 44
Sydney *64*
Tea 40, 60
Temples *34-5*, 38
Textiles 22, 26, 54
Thames river *12*
Tin 40, 44
Tobacco 40, 48
Tokyo 38, *38-9*
Tourism 16, 20, 58, 60
Tuareg people *57*
Unemployment 20
Uranium 60, 62, 64
Vancouver *42-3*
Vatican City 18
Vegetables 12, 22, 26, 28, 32, 38, 54, 66
Venice *19*, 20
Vesuvius, Mt 18
Victoria, Lake 60
Victoria Falls 62
Vikings 24
Volcanoes 18, *46*, 50
Volta river *59*
Wars 20, 26, 28, 32
Washington DC 46
Waterfalls 70
Wellington 66
Wheat 12, 30, 36, 42, 54
Wildlife *35*, *50*, 60, *61*, 66, 68, *68*, 69, *69*
Wines 14, *14*, 16, 18, 20
Yucatan peninsula *49*
Zaire river 60
Zimbabwe, Great *63*

Map Index

Aachen 27
Aare river 27
Aarhus 25
Abadan 33
Aberdeen 13
Abidjan 59
Abilene 45
Abu Dhabi 9, 33
Acapulco 48
Accra 59
Aconcagua 55
Adana 33
Addis Ababa 57
Adelaide 65
Aden 33
Aden, Gulf of 33
Adriatic Sea 19, 21
Aegean Sea 21
Afghanistan 9, 35
Africa 11, 56-63
Agra 35
Ahaggar Mts 57
Ahamadabad 35
Ajaccio 19
Ajmer 35
Akita 39
Alabama 45
Alaska 8, 42, 45, 68
Albania 8, 21
Albany, Australia 64
Albany, USA 45
Albany river 43
Alberta 42
Alborg 25
Albufeira 17
Albuquerque 44
Aleppo 33
Alexandria 57
Algarve Coast 17
Algeria 8, 56-7
Algiers 57
Alicante 17
Alice Springs 65
Allahabad 35
Aller river 27
Alma Ata 31
Almeria 17
Alps 15, 27
Altai Mts 37
Altyn Tagh Mts 37
Amarillo 45
Amazon river 51, 53
American Samoa (US) 67
Amiens 15
Amman 33
Amritsar 35
Amsterdam 23
Amundsen Sea 69
Amur river 31
Anchorage 45
Andalucia 17
Andaman Islands 41
Andes Mts 51, 53, 55
Andorra 15, 17
Andorra la Vella 17
Angel Falls 53
Angers 15
Angola 9, 63
Ankara 33
Annapolis 45
Anshan 37
Antananarivo 63
Antarctica 10-11, 69
Antarctic Circle 69
Antarctic Peninsula 69
Antigua 49
Antilles 49
Antofagasta 55
Antwerp 23
Aomori 39
Apajos river 53
Apeldoorn 23
Apennines 19
Appalachian Mts 45
Arabian Sea 33, 35

Arafura Sea 65
Aral Sea 31
Ararat, Mt 33
Arctic 10-11, 68
Arctic Circle 68
Arctic Ocean 11, 25, 30, 68
Ardennes 23
Arequipa 51
Argentina 8, 55
Arica 55
Arizona 44
Arkansas 45
Arkansas river 44-5
Arkhangelsk 30
Arles 15
Armenia 30
Arnhem 23
Arnhem Land 65
Asahigawa 39
Ashburton river 64
Asia 11, 31-41
Askhabad 30
Asmara 57
Assisi 19
Astrakhan 30
Asuncion 55
Aswan 57
Atacama Desert 55
Atbara 57
Atbara river 57
Athabaska, Lake 43
Athens 21
Atlanta 45
Atlantic Ocean 10, 13, 17, 25, 43, 45, 49, 53, 55, 56, 59, 63, 68
Atlas Mts 56
Auckland 67
Augsburg 27
Augusta 45
Austin 45
Australia 9, 11, 64-5, 67
Australian Alps 65
Austria 8, 27
Avignon 15
Avon river 13
Ayers Rock 65
Ayr 13
Azerbaijan 30
Baffin Bay 43, 68
Baffin Island 43, 68
Baghdad 33
Bahamas 8, 49
Bahia Blanca 55
Bahrain 8, 33
Baikal, Lake 31
Baja (Lower) California 48
Baku 30
Balaton, Lake 29
Balearic Islands 17
Bali 41
Balkan Mts 21
Balkans 21
Balkhash, Lake 31
Ballarat 65
Baltic Sea 19, 25, 27, 29
Baltimore 45
Bamako 57
Bandar Seri Begawan 41
Banda Sea 41
Bandjarmasin 41
Bandung 41
Bangalore 35
Bangkok 41
Bangladesh 9, 35
Bangor 45
Bangui 61
Bangweulu, Lake 63
Banjul 59
Banks Island 43, 68
Baotou 37
Barbados 8, 49
Barbuda and Antigua 49
Barcelona 17
Barents Sea 68
Bari 19

Barranquilla 51
Barrow river 13
Basel 27
Basra 33
Bath 13
Baton Rouge 45
Bayonne 15
Beaufort Sea 43, 68
Begawan 41
Beijing (Peking) 37
Beira 63
Beirut 33
Belem 53
Belfast 13
Belgium 8, 23
Belgrade 21
Belize 9, 49
Bellingshausen Sea 69
Belmopan 49
Belo Horizonte 53
Benares 35
Bendigo 65
Bengal, Bay of 35
Benghazi 57
Benguela 63
Benin 8, 59
Beni river 51
Ben Nevis 13
Benue river 59
Bergen 25
Bering Strait 68
Berlin 27
Besancon 15
Berne 27
Bhopal 35
Bhutan 9, 35
Bialystok 29
Biarritz 15
Bielefeld 27
Bilbao 17
Billings 44
Birmingham, England 13
Birmingham, USA 45
Biscay, Bay of 15
Bismarck 45
Bissau 59
Black Forest 27
Blackpool 13
Black Sea 31, 33
Blanc, Mt 15
Blantyre 63
Blenheim 67
Bloemfontein 63
Blue Nile river 57
Bochum 27
Bodensee 27
Bogota 51
Boise 44
Bolivia 8, 51
Bologna 19
Bolzano 19
Bombay 35
Bonn 27
Boras 25
Bordeaux 15
Bosnia Herzegovina 21
Boston 45
Bothnia, Gulf of 25
Botswana 9, 63
Boulogne 15
Bournemouth 13
Bradford 13
Braga 17
Brahmaputra river 35, 37
Brandon 43
Brasilia 53
Brasov 21
Bratislava 29
Brazil 8, 53
Brazilian Highlands 53
Brazzaville 59
Breda 23
Bremen 27
Bremerhaven 27

Brescia 19
Brest 15
Brighton 13
Brindisi 19
Brisbane 65
Bristol 13
British Columbia 42
British Isles 13
Brno 29
Broken Hill 65
Broome 65
Bruce, Mt 64
Bruges 23
Brunei 9, 41
Brunswick 27
Brussels 23
Bucaramanga 51
Bucharest 21
Budapest 29
Buenos Aires 55
Buffalo 45
Bug river 29
Bujumbura 61
Bukhara 31
Bulawayo 63
Bulgaria 9, 21
Burgas 21
Burgos 17
Burgundy 15
Burkina Faso 9, 59
Burma see Myanmar
Burundi 9, 61
Bydgoszcz 33
Byelorussia 30
Byrd Land 69
Cabinda 63
Cadiz 17
Caen 15
Cagliari 19
Cairns 65
Cairo 57
Calais 15
Calcutta 35
Calgary 42
Cali 51
Calicut 35
California 44
California, Gulf of 48
Callao 51
Camaguey 49
Cambodia (Kampuchea) 9, 41
Cambrian Mts 13
Cambridge 13
Cameroon 9, 59
Canada 8, 42-3, 68
Canary Islands 56
Canberra 65
Cancer, Tropic of 8
Cannes 15
Canterbury 13
Cape Canaveral 45
Cape Cod 45
Cape of Good Hope 63
Cape Horn 55
Cape Town 63
Cape Verde Islands 8
Cape York Peninsula 65
Capri 19
Capricorn, Tropic of 8
Caracas 53
Carcassonne 15
Cardiff 13
Caribbean Sea 49
Carnarvon 64
Caroline Islands 67
Caroni river 53
Carpathian Mts 21, 29
Carpentaria, Gulf of 65
Carson City 44
Cartagena, Colombia 51
Casablanca 56
Cascade Range 44-5
Casper 44
Caspian Sea 31, 33
Catania 19

Caucasus Mts 30
Cayenne 53
Cebu 41
Celebes Sea 41
Central Africa 61
Central African Republic 9, 61
Central America 6, 48-9
Central Plains (Eire) 13
Ceram 41
Cevennes Mts 15
Chad 9, 57
Chad, Lake 57
Champagne 15
Chang Jiang (Yangtze) river 37
Changsha 37
Channel Islands 13, 15
Chao Phraya river 41
Chari river 57
Charleroi 23
Charleston, South Carolina 45
Charleston, West Virginia 45
Charlotte 45
Charlottetown 43
Chartres 15
Chattanooga 45
Chelyabinsk 31
Chengdu 37
Cherbourg 15
Cheyenne 45
Chiba 39
Chicago 45
Chiclayo 51
Chihuahua 48
Chile 8, 55
Chiltern Hills 13
Chimbote 51
China 9, 37
Chiquicamata 55
Chittagong 35
Chongqing (Chungking) 37
Christchurch 67
Christmas Island 67
Churchill 43
Churchill river 43
Cienfuegos 49
Cincinnati 45
Cita 31
Clermont-Ferrand 15
Cleveland 45
Clipperton Islands 67
Cluj 21
Clyde river 13
Coast Ranges 44
Coats Land 69
Cochabamba 51
Cochin 35
Coimbra 17
Cologne 27
Colombia 8, 51
Colombo 35
Colorado 45
Colorado river, Argentina 55
Colorado river, USA 45
Colorado Springs 45
Columbia 45
Columbia river 44
Columbus, Georgia 45
Columbus, Ohio 45
Como, Lake 19
Comodoro Rivadavia 55
Comoros 63
Conakry 59
Concepcion 55
Concord 45
Congo 9, 59
Congo river see Zaire river
Connecticut 45
Constance, Lake 27
Constanta 21
Constantine see Qacentina
Continents 10-11
Cook Mt 67
Cook Islands 67
Cooper river 65
Copenhagen 25

Coral Sea 67
Cordoba, Argentina 55
Cordoba, Spain 17
Corfu 21
Corinth 21
Cork 13
Corpus Christi 45
Corsica 15, 19
Costa Rica 9, 49
Cote d'Ivoire (Ivory Coast) 8, 59
Cotswolds 13
Cottbus 27
Coventry 13
Craiova 21
Crete 21
Croatia 21
Cuando river 63
Cuanza river 63
Cuba 8, 49
Cubango river 63
Culiacan 48
Cunene river 63
Curitiba 53
Cuttack 35
Cuzco 51
Cyprus 8, 33
Czechoslovakia 8, 29
Dakar 59
Dalian (Luda) 37
Dallas 45
Dal river 25
Daly river 65
Damascus 33
Dampier 64
Da Nang 41
Danube river 21, 27, 29
Dar-es-Salaam 61
Darfur Mts 57
Darjeeling 35
Darling Range 64
Darling river 65
Darmstadt 27
Dartmoor 13
Darwin 65
Davao 41
Davenport 45
Dawson 42
Dead Sea 33
Debrecen 29
Deccan Plateau 35
Dee river 13
Delaware 45
Delhi 35
Delphi 21
Denmark 8, 25
Denver 45
Derg, Lough 13
Des Moines 45
Dessau 27
Detroit 45
Devon Island 43
Dhaka 35
Diamantina river 65
Dieppe 15
Dijon 15
Dinaric Alps 21
Djibouti 9, 61
Dnieper river 30
Dodoma 61
Doha 33
Dominica 8, 49
Dominican Republic 9, 49
Donetsk 30
Don river 30
Dordogne river 15
Dordrecht 23
Dore, Mt 15
Dortmund 27
Douai 15
Douala 59
Douro river 17
Dover, England 13
Dover, USA 45
Drakensberg 63
Drava river 21

Dresden 27
Dubai 33
Dublin 13
Dubrovnik 21
Duero river 17
Duisburg 27
Dundee 13
Dunedin 67
Dunfermline 13
Dunkerque 15
Durban 63
Durres 21
Dusseldorf 27
East Africa 61
East China Sea 37
Easter Island 67
Eastern Europe 29
Eastern Ghats 35
East London 63
East Siberian Sea 31, 68
Ebro river 17
Ecuador 8, 51
Eden river 13
Edinburgh 13
Edmonton 42
Egmont Mt 67
Egypt 9, 57
Eindhoven 23
Elbe river 27, 29
Elbrus, Mt 30
Elburz Mts 33
Ellesmere Island 68
Ellsworth Land 69
El Misti 51
El Paso 44
El Salvador 9, 49
Ems river 27
Enderby Land 69
England 13
English Channel 13, 15
Enns river 27
Enschede 23
Enugu 59
Equator 8
Equatorial Guinea 9, 59
Erfurt 27
Erie, Lake 43, 45
Eritrea 57
Esbjerg 25
Esfahan 33
Eskilstuna 25
Essen 27
Estonia 9, 30
Ethiopia 9, 57
Etna, Mt 19
Eucla 65
Euphrates river 33
Europe 8-9, 11, 12-30
Evansville 45
Everest, Mt 35
Exeter 13
Exmoor 13
Eyre, Lake 65
Fairbanks 42
Faisalabad 35
Falkland Islands 8, 55
Faro 17
Fens, The 13
Ferrara 19
Fez 56
Fiji 9, 67
Finland 9, 25, 68
Finland, Gulf of 25
Fishguard 13
Flinders Island 65
Flinders Ranges 65
Flinders river 65
Florence 19
Flores 41
Flores Sea 41
Florida 45
Florida, Straits of 49
Fontainebleau 15
Fortaleza 53
Fort Lauderdale 45

Fort Rupert 43
Fort Smith 45
Fort Worth 45
France 8, 15
Frankfort 45
Frankfurt 27
Franz Josef Land 31, 68
Fredericton 43
Freetown 59
Freiburg 27
Fremantle 64
French Alps 15
French Guiana 9, 53
French Polynesia 67
Frisian Islands 23
Frunze 31
Fuji, Mt 39
Fukuoka 39
Fushun 37
Fuzhou 37
Gabon 9, 59
Gaborone 63
Galapagos Islands 67
Galati 21
Gallivare 25
Galway 13
Gambia, The 9, 59
Gambia river 59
Ganges river 35
Gannett Peak 44
Garda, Lake 19
Garonne river 15
Gascoyne river 64
Gavle 25
Gaza Strip 33
Gdansk 29
Geelong 65
Geneva 27
Geneva, Lake see Leman, Lake
Genoa 19
Georgetown 53
Georgia 30
Georgia, USA 45
Georgina river 65
Gera 27
Geraldton 64
Germany 8, 27
Ghana 8, 59
Ghent 23
Gibraltar 17
Gibson Desert 64-5
Gijon 17
Gisborne 67
Giza 57
Glama river 25
Glasgow 13
Glittertind, Mt 25
Glommen river 25
Goa 35
Gobi Desert 37
Godavari river 35
Godthaab 68
Goiania 53
Golan Heights 33
Gold Coast 65
Gorki 30
Goteborg 25
Gotland 25
Grampians 13
Granada 17
Gran Chaco 55
Grand Canyon 44
Grand Rapids 45
Grand Teton 44
Graz 27
Great Australian Bight 65
Great Barrier Reef 65
Great Bear Lake 42
Great Britain 13
Great Dividing Range 65
Greater Antilles 49
Great Falls 44
Great Salt Desert 33
Great Salt Lake 44
Great Sand Desert 33

Great Sandy Desert 65
Great Slave Lake 43
Great Victoria Desert 65
Great Wall of China 37
Great Yarmouth 13
Greece 9, 21
Greenland 8, 68
Greenland Sea 68
Grenada 49
Grenoble 15
Greymouth 67
Groningen 23
Groote Eylandt 65
Gross Glockner 27
Guadalajara 48
Guadalquivir river 17
Guadeloupe 49
Guadiana river 17
Guangzhou (Canton) 37
Guatemala 9, 49
Guatemala City 49
Guayaquil 51
Guiana Highlands 53
Guinea 9, 59
Guinea-Bissau 9, 59
Guiyang 37
Guyana 9, 53
Gyor 29
Haarlem 23
Hague, The 23
Hainan 37
Haiphong 41
Haiti 9, 49
Hakodate 39
Halifax 43
Halle 27
Halmahera 41
Halmstad 25
Halsingborg 25
Hamamatsu 39
Hamburg 27
Hamilton, Canada 43
Hamilton, New Zealand 67
Hammerfest 25
Hangzhou 37
Hanoi 41
Hanover 27
Harare 63
Harbin 37
Hardanger fiord 25
Harrisburg 45
Hartford 45
Harz Mts 27
Havana 49
Hawaii 45, 67
Hebrides 13
Heerlen-Kerkrase 23
Hekla, Mt 25
Helena 44
Helmand river 35
Helsinki 25
Herat 35
Hermosillo 48
Highlands, Scotland 13
Himalayas 35, 37
Hindu Kush 35
Hiroshima 39
Hobart 65
Ho Chi Minh City (Saigon) 41
Hohhot 37
Hokkaido 39
Holguin 49
Honduras 9, 49
Honduras, Gulf of 49
Hong Kong 9, 37
Honolulu 45, 67
Honshu 39
Houston 45
Huambo 63
Huancayo 51
Huang He river 37
Hudson Bay 43, 68
Hudson Strait 43
Hue 41
Huelva 17

Hull 134
Hungary 8, 29
Huron, Lake 43, 45
Hyderabad 35
Iasi 21
Ibadan 59
Ibiza 17
Iceland 8, 25, 68
Idaho 44
IJsselmeer 23
IJssel river 23
Illinois 45
India 9, 35
Indiana 45
Indianapolis 45
Indian Ocean 11, 41, 35, 61, 63, 64, 69
Indonesia 9, 41
Indore 35
Indus river 35
Inner Mongolia 37
Inn river 27
Innsbruck 27
Invercargill 67
Inverness 13
Ionian Sea 21
Iowa 45
Ipswich 13
Iquique 55
Iquitos 51
Iraklion 21
Iran 9, 33
Iraq 9, 33
Ireland, Northern 8, 13
Ireland, Republic of (Eire) 8, 13
Irian Jaya (Indonesia) 67
Irish Sea 13
Irkutsk 31
Irrawaddy river 41
Iskar river 21
Islamabad 35
Israel 8, 33
Istanbul 33
Italy 8, 19
Ivory Coast see Cote d'Ivoire
Iwaki 39
Izmir 33
Jackson 45
Jacksonville 45
Jaipur 35
Jakarta 41
Jamaica 9, 49
Jammu and Kashmir 35
Japan 9, 39
Japan, Sea of 31, 39
Java 41
Java Sea 41
Jeddah 33
Jefferson City 45
Jerusalem 33
Jilin 37
Jinan (Tsinan) 37
Joao Pessoa 53
Jodhpur 35
Johannesburg 63
Johnston Islands 67
Jonkoping 25
Jordan 8, 33
Jubbar river 61
Juneau 45
Jura Mts 15, 27
Jyvaskyla 25
K2 35
Kabul 35
Kaduna 59
Kagoshima 39
Kaitaia 67
Kalahari Desert 63
Kalamata 21
Kalgoorlie 64
Kalimantan 41
Kamchatka Peninsula 31
Kampala 61
Kampuchea see Cambodia
Kanazawa 39

73

Kanchenjunga, Mt 35
Kandahar 35
Kangaroo Island 65
Kano 59
Kanpur 35
Kansas 45
Kansas City 45
Kaohsiung 37
Karachi 35
Karakoram Range 35
Kara Kum Mts 30
Kara Sea 31
Kariba, Lake 63
Karl-Marx-Stadt 27
Karlsruhe 27
Karlstad 25
Kasai river 61
Kashmir see Jammu and Kashmir
Kassel 27
Katmandu 35
Katowice 29
Kattegat 25
Kauai 45
Kawasaki 39
Kazakhstan 31
Kenora 43
Kentucky 45
Kenya 9, 61
Kermadec Islands 67
Kerry, Mts of 13
Khabarovsk 31
Kharkov 30
Khartoum 57
Khirgizia 31
Khyber Pass 35
Kiel 27
Kiel Canal 27
Kiev 30
Kigali 61
Kilimanjaro, Mt 61
Kimberley 63
King Island 65
Kingston 49
Kinshasa 61
Kiribati Republic 67
Kirkwall 13
Kirov 30
Kiruna 25
Kisangani 61
Kishinev 30
Kismaju 61
Kitakyushu 39
Kitwe 63
Klar river 25
Kobe 39
Koblenz 27
Kolyma river 31
Korea see North Korea; South Korea
Kosice 29
Koszalin 29
Krakatoa 41
Krakow 29
Krefeld 27
Krishna river 35
Kristiansand 25
Kuala Lumpur 41
Kunlun Shan Mts 37
Kunming 37
Kuopio 25
Kuwait 8, 33
Kuwait City 33
Kuybyshev 30
Kyoto 39
Kyushu 39
Laayonne 56
Labrador 43
La Coruna 17
Lagen river 25
Lagos, Nigeria 59
Lagos, Portugal 17
Lahore 35
Lahti 25
Lake District 13
Lanchang Jiang (Mekong) river 37, 41

Land's End 13
Lansing 45
Lanzhou 37
Laos 9, 41
La Paz 51
Lapland 68
La Plata 55
Laptev Sea 31, 68
Larisa 21
Las Vegas 44
Latvia 9, 30
Launceston 65
Lausanne 27
Lebanon 8, 33
Leeds 13
Leeward Islands 49
Le Havre 15
Leicester 13
Leichhardt river 65
Leiden 23
Leipzig 27
Lek river 23
Leman, Lake 27
Le Mans 15
Lena river 31
Leon, Mexico 48
Lesotho 9, 63
Lesser Antilles 49
Lesvos 21
Lhasa 37
Liao river 37
Liberia 9, 59
Libreville 59
Libya 9, 57
Liechtenstein 27
Liege 23
Ligurian Sea 19
Lille 15
Lilongwe 63
Lima 51
Limerick 13
Limoges 15
Limpopo river 63
Lincoln 45
Linkoping 25
Linz 27
Lisbon 17
Lithuania 9, 30
Little Rock 45
Liverpool 13
Livorno 19
Ljubljana 21
Ljusnan river 25
Lobito 63
Lodz 29
Lofoten Islands 25
Logan, Mt 42
Loire river 15
Lome 59
Lomond, Loch 13
London 13
Londonderry 13
Long Island 45
Los Angeles 44
Louisiana 45
Louisville 45
Lourdes 15
Lualaba river 61
Luanda 63
Lubeck 27
Lublin 29
Lubumbashi 61
Lucerne 27
Lucknow 35
Lulea 25
Lule river 25
Lusaka 63
Luxembourg 8, 23
Luxor 57
Luyang 37
Luzon 41
Lyon 15
Lys river 23
Maas river 23
Maastricht 23

Macao 37
Macdonnell Range 65
Macedonia 21
Maceio 53
Mackenzie Mts 42
Mackenzie river 42
McKinley, Mt 44
Madagascar 9, 63
Madeira 56
Madeira river 51, 53
Madison 45
Madras 35
Madrid 17
Madurai 35
Magdalena river 51
Magdeburg 27
Maggiore, Lake 19
Mahajonja 63
Mahanadi river 35
Maiduguri 59
Maine 45
Main river 27
Mainz 27
Majorca 17
Malabo 59
Malaga 17
Malang 41
Malawi 9, 63
Malawi, Lake see Nyasa, Lake
Malaysia 9, 41
Maldive Islands 9
Mali 8, 56
Malmo 25
Malta 19
Man, Isle of 13
Managua 49
Manama 33
Manaus 53
Manchester 13
Manchuria 37
Mandalay 41
Manila 41
Manitoba 43
Mannheim 27
Manukau 67
Maputo 63
Maracaibo 53
Maracaibo, Lake 53
Maranon river 51
Marbella 17
Mar del Plata 55
Mariana Islands 67
Maritsa river 21
Marne river 15
Marquesas Islands 67
Marrakech 56
Marseille 15
Marshall Islands 67
Martinique 49
Maryland 45
Maseru 63
Mashhad 33
Mask, Lough 13
Massachusetts 45
Massif Central 15
Mato Grosso 53
Matsuyama 39
Matterhorn 27
Maui 45
Mauritania 8, 56
Mbabane 63
Mbuji-Mayi 61
Mecca 33
Medan 41
Medellin 51
Medina 33
Mediterranean Sea 15, 17, 19, 21, 33, 57
Meerut 35
Mekong river see Lanchang Jiang
Melbourne 65
Melville Island, Australia 65
Melville Island, Canada 43
Memphis 45
Mendoza 55

Merida 49
Mesopotamia 33
Messina 19
Metz 15
Meuse river 15, 23
Mexicali 48
Mexico 8, 48, 67
Mexico, Gulf of 45, 49
Mexico City 48
Miami 45
Michigan 45
Michigan, Lake 43, 45
Micronesia, Federated States of 67
Middle East 11, 33
Middlesborough 13
Midway Islands (US) 67
Milan 19
Milwaukee 45
Mindanao 41
Minneapolis 45
Minnesota 45
Minorca 17
Minsk 30
Miskolc 29
Mississippi 45
Mississippi river 45
Missouri 45
Missouri river 44-5
Mitchell river 65
Miyazaki 39
Mocambique 63
Modena 19
Mogadishu 61
Moldova 30
Molucca Islands 41
Mombasa 61
Monaco 19
Monchen-Gladbach 27
Mongolia 9, 37
Monroe 45
Monrovia 59
Mons 23
Montana 44
Montenegro 21
Monterrey 48
Montevideo 55
Montgomery 45
Montpelier, USA 45
Montpellier, France 15
Montreal 43
Morava river 21
Morocco 8, 56
Moscow 30
Mosel river 27
Mosul 33
Moulmein 41
Mount Isa 65
Mozambique 9, 63
Mozambique Channel 63
Mulhacen, Mt 17
Mulhouse 15
Munich 27
Munster 27
Murchison river 64
Murcia 17
Murmansk 30, 68
Murray river 65
Murrumbidgee river 65
Musala, Mt 21
Muscat 33
Musgrave Ranges 65
Mweru, Lake 63
Myanmar (Burma) 9, 41
Mykonos 21
Mysore 35
Nagasaki 39
Nagoya 39
Nagpur 35
Nairobi 61
Namib Desert 63
Namibia 9, 63
Namur 23
Nanchang 37
Nancy 15
Nanda Devi 35

Nanjing 37
Nanning 37
Nantes 15
Napier 67
Naples 19
Narbonne 15
Narmada river 35
Narvik 25
Nashville 45
Nassau 49
Nasser, Lake 57
Nauru 67
Naxos 21
N'Djamena 57
Ndola 63
Nebraska 45
Negro river 53, 55
Neisse river 27, 29
Nelson 67
Nelson river 43
Nepal 9, 35
Ness, Loch 13
Netherlands 8, 23
Netze river 29
Nevada 44
Newark 45
New Brunswick 43
New Caledonia 9, 67
Newcastle 65
Newcastle upon Tyne 13
New Delhi 35
Newfoundland 43
New Hampshire 45
New Jersey 45
New Mexico 44
New Orleans 45
New Plymouth 67
New Siberian Islands 31, 68
New South Wales 65
New York 45
New York City 45
New Zealand 9, 67
Niagara Falls 43
Niamey 57
Nicaragua 9, 49
Nicaragua, Lake 49
Nice 15
Nicobar Islands 41
Nicosia 33
Niger 8, 57
Nigeria 8, 59
Niger river 56, 59
Niigata 39
Nijmegen 23
Nile river 57
Nimes 15
Nipigon, Lake 43
Nis 21
Norfolk, USA 45
Norrkoping 25
North Africa 8-9, 56-7
North America 10, 42-7
North Carolina 45
North Dakota 45
North Downs 13
Northern Ireland 13
Northern Territory 65
North Korea 9, 37
North Platte river 44-5
North Pole 68
North Sea 13, 15, 19, 23, 25, 27
North West Highlands 13
Northwest Territories 42-3
Norway 9, 25, 68
Norwegian Sea 30
Norwich 13
Nottingham 13
Nouakchott 56
Nova Scotia 43
Novaya Zemlya 31, 68
Novosibirsk 31
Nu Jiang (Salween) river 37, 41
Nullarbor Plain 64-5
Nuremberg 27
Nyasa, Lake 63

Nyiregyhaza 29
Oahu 45
Oakland 44
Oban 13
Ob river 31
Oceania 7, 64-3
Odense 25
Oder river 27, 29
Odessa 30
Offenbach 27
Ohio 45
Ohio river 45
Oise river 15
Okavango Swamps 63
Okayama 39
Okhotsk, Sea of 31, 39
Oklahoma 45
Oklahoma City 45
Oldenburg 27
Olympia, Greece 21
Olympia, USA 44
Olympus, Mt 21
Omaha 45
Oman 9, 33
Omdurman 57
Omsk 31
Ontario 43
Ontario, Lake 43, 45
Oporto 17
Oran 56
Orange river 63
Ord river 65
Orebro 25
Oregon 44
Orinoco river 53
Orkney Islands 13
Orlando 45
Orleans 15
Osaka 39
Oslo 25
Osorno 55
Ostend 23
Ostrava 29
Ottawa 43
Ouagoudougou 59
Oubangui river 59
Oulu 25
Ouse river 13
Oviedo 17
Oxford 13
Pacific Ocean 10, 11, 37, 39, 41, 44, 48, 51, 53, 55, 65, 67, 68
Padua 19
Pakistan 9, 35
Palau (Trust territory) 67
Palawan 41
Palembang 41
Palermo 19
Palma 17
Palmer Land 69
Palmerston North 67
Palmyra Islands 67
Pamir Mts 31, 35
Pampas 55
Pamplona 17
Panama 9, 49
Panama Canal 49
Panama City 49
Papua New Guinea 9, 67
Paraguay 8, 55
Paraguay river 53
Paramaribo 53
Parana river 53, 55
Paris 15
Parma 19
Parramatta 65
Patagonia 55
Patna 35
Patras 21
Pecs 29
Pembar 61
Pennines 13
Pennsylvania 45
Penzance 13
Perigueux 15

Perm 30
Perpignan 15
Persian Gulf 33
Perth, Australia 64
Perth, Scotland 13
Peru 8, 51
Perugia 19
Philadelphia 45
Philippines 9, 41
Phnom-Penh 41
Phoenix 44
Phoenix Islands 67
Pierre 45
Pikes Peak 44
Pindus Mts 21
Piraeus 21
Pisa 19
Pitcairn Island 67
Pittsburgh 45
Piura 51
Platte river 44-5
Ploesti 21
Plovdiv 21
Plymouth 13
Plzen 29
Poland 9, 29
Polar regions 68-9
Pontianak 41
Poona 35
Poopo, Lake 51
Popacatapetl, Mt 48
Pori 25
Po river 19
Port-au-Prince 49
Port Elizabeth 63
Port Harcourt 59
Port Hedland 64
Portland, Maine 45
Portland, Oregon 44
Port Lincoln 65
Port Moresby 67
Porto Alegre 53
Port-of-Spain 53
Porto Novo 59
Portsmouth 13
Port Sudan 57
Portugal 8, 17
Poznan 29
Prague 29
Pretoria 63
Prince Edward Island 43
Prince George 42
Providence 45
Puebla 49
Pueblo 45
Puerto Montt 55
Puerto Rico 9, 49
Punta Arenas 55
Purus river 53
Pusan 37
Pyongyang 37
Pyrenees 15, 17
Qacentina (Constantine) 57
Qatar 9, 33
Qattara Depression 57
Qingdao 37
Qiqihar 37
Quebec 43
Queen Elizabeth Islands 43, 68
Queen Maud Land 69
Queensland 65
Quezon City 41
Quito 51
Rabat 56
Rainier, Mt 44
Raleigh 45
Rangoon 41
Rapid City 45
Ras Dashen, Mt 57
Rawalpindi 35
Reading 13
Recife 53
Red river 44-5
Red Sea 33, 57, 61
Regensburg 27

Reggio 19
Regina 43
Reims 15
Rennes 15
Reno 44
Revilla Gigedo Islands 67
Reykjavik 25, 68
Rhine river 23, 27
Rhode Island 45
Rhodes 21
Rhodope Mts 21
Rhone river 15, 27
Richmond 45
Riga 30
Rijeka 21
Rimini 19
Rio de Janeiro 53
Rio Gallegos 55
Rio Grande river 45, 48
Riyadh 33
Rockhampton 65
Rocky Mts 42, 44
Romania 9, 21
Rome 19
Roper river 65
Rosario 55
Ross Ice Shelf 69
Ross Sea 69
Rostock 27
Rotorua 67
Rotterdam 23
Roubaix 15
Rouen 15
Rub'al Khali (Empty Quarter) 33
Ruhr river 27
Ruse 21
Russia 9, 30-1
Ruwenzori Range 61
Rwanda 9, 61
Saarbrucken 27
Sabah 41
Sacramento 44
Sacramento river 44
Sahara Desert 57
Saint-Etienne 15
St Helens, Mt 44
St John's 43
St Kitts Nevis 49
St Lawrence river 43
St Louis 45
St Lucia 8, 49
St Paul 45
St Petersburg 30
St Vincent 49
Salado river 55
Salamanca 17
Salem 44
Salerno 19
Salt Lake City 44
Salvador 53
Salween river see Nu Jiang
Salzburg 27
Samarkand 31
San'a 33
San Antonio 45
San Diego 44
San Francisco 44
San Joaquin river 44
San Jose, Costa Rica 49
San Jose, USA 44
San Juan, Argentina 55
San Juan, Puerto Rico 49
San Luis Potosi 48
San Marino 19
San Salvador 49
San Sebastian 17
Santa Clara 49
Santa Cruz 51
Santa Fe, Argentina 55
Santa Fe, USA 45
Santander 17
Santiago 55
Santiago de Compostella 17
Santiago de Cuba 49
Santo Domingo 49

Santos 53
Sao Francisco river 53
Sao Luis 53
Saone river 15
Sao Paulo 53
Sao Tome and Principe 59
Sapporo 39
Sarajevo 21
Sarawak 41
Sardinia 19
Saskatchewan 43
Saskatchewan river 43
Saskatoon 43
Sassari 19
Saudi Arabia 9, 33
Sault Ste Marie 43
Savannah 45
Sava river 21
Scandinavia 11, 25
Schelde river 23
Schwerin 27
Scilly Isles 13
Scotland 13
Seattle 44
Segovia 17
Segura river 17
Seine river 15
Semarang 41
Sendai 39
Senegal 9, 59
Senegal river 56, 59
Seoul 37
Serbia 21
Setubal 17
Sevastopol 30
Severnaya Zemlya 31
Severn river 13
Seville 17
Seychelles 9
Sfax 57
Shanghai 37
Shannon river 13
Shebele river 61
Sheffield 13
Shenyang 37
's-Hertogenbosch 23
Shetland Islands 13
Shikoku 39
Shiraz 33
Shizuoka 39
Siberia 31
Sicily 19
Siegen 27
Siena 19
Sierra Leone 9, 59
Sierra Madre del Sur 48
Sierra Madre Occidental 48
Sierra Madre Oriental 48
Sierra Nevada, Spain 17
Sierra Nevada, USA 44
Si-Kiang river 37
Sikkim 35
Simpson Desert 65
Singapore 9, 41
Sioux City 45
Skagerrak 25
Skelleftea 25
Skien 25
Skopje 21
Sligo 13
Slovenia 21
Snake river 44
Snowdon 13
Society Islands 67
Sofia 21
Sogne Fiord 25
Solomon Islands 9, 67
Somalia 9, 61
Somme river 15
Songea 61
South Africa 9, 63
South America 10, 50-5
Southampton 13
South Atlantic Ocean 69
South Australia 65

South Carolina 45
South China Sea 37, 39, 41
South Dakota 45
South Downs 13
Southeast Asia 11, 41
Southern Alps 67
South Korea 9, 37
South Pacific Ocean 69
South Platte river 44-5
South Pole 69
Southport, Australia 65
Spain 8, 17
Sparta 21
Split 21
Spokane 44
Spree river 27
Springfield, Illinois 45
Springfield, Missouri 45
Sri Lanka 9, 35
Srinagar 35
Stavanger 25
Stewart Island 67
Stockholm 25
Stoke-on-Trent 13
Strasbourg 15
Stromboli 19
Stuttgart 27
Sucre 51
Sudan 9, 57
Sudbury 43
Suez 57
Suez Canal 57
Sulawesi (Celebes) 41
Sulu Sea 41
Sumatra 41
Sumba 41
Sumbawa 41
Sundsvall 25
Superior, Lake 43, 45
Surabaya 41
Surakarta 41
Surat 35
Surinam 9, 53
Sutlej river 35
Svalbard 68
Sverdlovsk 31
Swansea 13
Swaziland 9, 63
Sweden 9, 25, 68
Switzerland 8, 27
Sydney 65
Syracuse, Sicily 19
Syracuse, USA 45
Syria 8, 33
Szczecin 29
Szeged 29
Tabriz 33
Tagus river 17
Taipei 37
Taiwan 9, 37
Taiyuan 37
Tajikistan 31
Talca 55
Tallahassee 45
Tallinn 30
Tampa 45
Tampere 25
Tampico 49
Tana, Lake 57
Tanganyika, Lake 61
Tangier 56
Tangshan 37
Tanzania 9, 61
Tapajos river 53
Taranto 19
Tarim Basin 37
Tarragona 17
Tashkent 31
Tasmania 65
Tasman Sea 65, 67
Taupo, Lake 67
Tay river 13
Tbilisi 30
Tegucigalpa 49
Tehran 33

75

Tel Aviv-Yafo 33
Temuco 55
Tennant Creek 65
Tennessee 45
Tennessee river 45
Texas 45
Thailand 9, 41
Thailand, Gulf of 37, 41
Thames river 13
Thar Desert 35
Thessaloniki 21
Thimbu 35
Thule 68
Thunder Bay 43
Tianjin (Tientsin) 37
Tiber river 19
Tibesti Mts 57
Tibet 37
Tien Shan Mts 31, 37
Tierra del Fuego 55
Tigris river 33
Tijuana 48
Tilburg 23
Timaru 67
Timbuktu 56
Timisoara 21
Timor 41
Timor Sea 41, 65
Tirana 21
Tisa river 21
Tisza river 29
Titicaca, Lake 51
Tobago *see* Trinidad and Tobago
Tocantins river 53
Togo 9, 59
Tokyo 39
Toledo, Spain 17
Toledo, USA 45
Toliara 63
Tomsk 31
Tonga 67
Toowoomba 65
Topeka 45
Torne river 25

Toronto 43
Torrens, Lake 65
Toulon 15
Toulouse 15
Tours 15
Townsville 65
Transylvania Alps 21
Trenton 45
Trent river 13
Trieste 19
Triglav, Mt 21
Trinidad and Tobago 9, 49, 53
Tripoli 57
Trivandrum 35
Trois Rivieres 43
Tromso 25
Trondheim 25
Trujillo 51
Tsangpao (Brahmaputra) river 37
Tuamotu Islands 67
Tucson 44
Tucuman 55
Tulsa 45
Tunis 57
Tunisia 9, 57
Turin 19
Turkana, Lake 61
Turkey 9, 33
Turkmenistan 30-1
Turku 25
Turnu Severin 21
Tuvalu 67
Tyne river 13
Tyrrhenian Sea 19
Uganda 9, 61
Ujung Pandang 41
Ukraine 30
Ulan Bator 37
Umea 25
Ume river 25
Union of Soviet Socialist Republics, former 9, 30-1, 68
United Arab Emirates 8, 33
United Kingdom 8, 13

United States of America 8, 44-5
Uppsala 25
Ural Mts 31
Ural river 30
Uruguay 8, 55
Uruguay river 55
Urumqi 37
Utah 44
Utrecht 23
Uzbekistan 30-1
Vaal river 63
Vaasa 25
Vaduz 27
Valdivia 55
Valencia 17
Valenciennes 15
Valetta 19
Valladolid 17
Valparaiso 55
Vancouver 42
Vancouver Island 42
Vanern, Lake 25
Van river 29, 33
Vanuatu Republic 9, 67
Varanasi 35
Varanger Fiord 25
Vardar river 21
Varna 21
Vasteras 25
Vatican City 19
Vattern, Lake 25
Venezuela 8, 53
Venice 19
Veracruz 49
Vermont 45
Verona 19
Versailles 15
Vesuvius, Mt 19
Victoria, Australia 65
Victoria, Canada 42
Victoria, Lake 61
Victoria Falls 63
Victoria Island 43, 68
Victoria Land 69

Victoria river 65
Vienna 27
Vientiane 41
Vietnam 9, 41
Vigo 17
Vilnius 30
Virginia 45
Vistula river 29
Vladivostok 31
Vltava river 29
Volga river 30
Volgograd 30
Volta, Lake 59
Vosges Mts 15
Vulcano 19
Waal river 23
Waddenzee 23
Wagga Wagga 65
Wakayama 39
Wake Island 67
Wales 13
Wallis and Futuna 67
Walvis Bay 63
Wanganui 67
Wanneroo 64
Warsaw 29
Warta river 21
Washington 44
Washington, DC 45
Waterford 13
Weddell Sea 69
Wellesley Island 65
Wellington 67
Weser river 27
West Africa 58-9
West Bank 33
Western Australia 64-5
Western Ghats 35
Western Sahara 56
Western Samoa 67
West Virginia 45
Whitehorse 42
White Nile river 57
Whitney, Mt 44

Whyalla 65
Wichita 45
Wicklow Mts 13
Wiesbaden 27
Wight, Isle of 13
Windhoek 63
Windward Islands 49
Winnipeg 43
Winnipeg, Lake 43
Wisconsin 45
Wollongong 65
Wroclaw 29
Wuhan 37
Wuppertal 27
Wurzburg 27
Wyoming 44
Xi'an 37
Xingu river 53
Xuzhou 37
Yangtze river *see* Chang Jiang
Yaounde 59
Yellowknife 42
Yellow Sea 37
Yemen 9, 33
Yenisei river 31
Yerevan 30
Yichang 37
Yokohama 39
York 13
Yucatan Peninsula 49
Yugoslavia 8, 21
Yukon river 42
Yukon Territory 42
Zagreb 21
Zagros Mts 33
Zaire 9, 61
Zaire river 61
Zambezi river 63
Zambia 9, 63
Zanzibar 61
Zaragoza 17
Zhengzhou 37
Zimbabwe 9, 63
Zurich 27

ACKNOWLEDGEMENTS

The publishers wish to thank the following for supplying photographs for this book:

Page 12 ZEFA; 14 ZEFA (top), Helene Rogers/Trip (bottom); 16 ZEFA (top), Spectrum (bottom); 18 Keith Horn (top), ZEFA (bottom); 20 Eye Ubiquitous (top), ZEFA (bottom); 22 ZEFA; 24 Finnish Tourist Board (top), ZEFA (bottom); 26 The Hutchison Library (top), ZEFA (bottom); 28 Sefton Photo Library (top), ZEFA (bottom); 30 ZEFA; 31 The Hutchison Library; 32 Christine Osborne Pictures; 34 The Hutchison Library (top), J. Cleare Mountain Camera (centre), ZEFA (bottom); 36 ZEFA; 37 The Hutchison Library; 38 The Hutchison Library; 40 ZEFA; 42 ZEFA (left), A.R. Dajon (right); 44 ZEFA; 46 ZEFA; 49 D. Saunders/Trip (top), Helene Rogers/Trip (bottom); 50 Eye Ubiquitous; 51 Life File/Trip; 52 ZEFA; 54 ZEFA (top right), D. Saunders/Trip (left and bottom right); 57 ZEFA; 59 Panos Pictures (left), Life File/Trip (right); 60 D. Saunders/Trip (top), Spectrum Colour Library (bottom); 62 ZEFA (top right), D. Saunders/Trip (bottom left); 64 ZEFA (left), Eye Ubiquitous (right); 66 ZEFA (left), Spectrum Colour Library (right); 70 J. Allan Cash Photo Library (left), John Cleare (right).

Picture Research
Elaine Willis and Su Alexander